T0045878

To:

....

From:

....

DEVOTIONS

from the MOUNTAINS

DEVOTIONS

from the MOUNTAINS

by LISA HAM

THOMAS NELSON

Since 1798

Devotions from the Mountains

© 2017 Thomas Nelson

All rights reserved. No portion of this book may be reproduced, stored in a retrieval system, or transmitted in any form or by any means–electronic, mechanical, photocopy, recording, scanning, or other–except for brief quotations in critical reviews or articles, without the prior written permission of the publisher.

Published in Nashville, Tennessee, by Thomas Nelson. Thomas Nelson is a registered trademark of HarperCollins Christian Publishing, Inc.

Interior photos: Shutterstock

Unless otherwise noted, Scripture quotations are taken from the Holy Bible, New International Version®, NIV®. Copyright © 1973, 1978, 1984, 2011 by Biblica, Inc.® Used by permission of Zondervan. All rights reserved worldwide. www.Zondervan.com. The "NIV" and "New International Version" are trademarks registered in the United States Patent and Trademark Office by Biblica, Inc.®

Scripture quotations marked AMP are from the Amplified® Bible. Copyright © 1954, 1958, 1962, 1964, 1965, 1987 by The Lockman Foundation. Used by permission. (www.Lockman.org)

Scripture quotations marked ESV are from the ESV® Bible (The Holy Bible, English Standard Version®). Copyright © 2001 by Crossway, a publishing ministry of Good News Publishers. Used by permission. All rights reserved.

Scripture quotations marked KJV are from the King James Version. Public domain.

Scripture quotations marked NASB are from New American Standard Bible®. Copyright © 1960, 1962, 1963, 1968, 1971, 1972, 1973, 1975, 1977, 1995 by The Lockman Foundation. Used by permission. (www.Lockman.org)

Any Internet addresses, phone numbers, or company or product information printed in this book are offered as a resource and are not intended in any way to be or to imply an endorsement by Thomas Nelson, nor does Thomas Nelson vouch for the existence, content, or services of these sites, phone numbers, companies, or products beyond the life of this book.

ISBN 978-0-7180-9065-4 (eBook)
ISBN 978-0-7180-8685-5 (HC)

Printed in Malaysia

24 25 26 OFF 11 10 9 8

CONTENTS

A HIGHER PERSPECTIVE

"For my thoughts are not your thoughts, neither are your ways my ways,"
declares the LORD. "As the heavens are higher than the earth, so are my
ways higher than your ways and my thoughts than your thoughts."

ISAIAH 55:8–9

The mountains offer us a chance to see the world afresh. Whether we hike or drive, take a chairlift or snowmobile, we get away, breathe fresh air, and see the view. From high on a mountain, the world looks very different. We can see so much more. Roads dwindle into the distance, and cities look like toy models, if we can glimpse them at all. Faraway hills and peaks may take some work to identify as we see them from a new angle. The landscape stretches out before us, and we gain perspective. Breathing room. Our minds clear a bit. We get some distance, literally and figuratively, from all the things that stress us out. We are calmed. We breathe easier. Our nerves are soothed.

As stunning as that change of viewpoint is, it's nothing at all compared to the difference between God's thoughts and our thoughts. He sees everything, knows everything, understands everything. His thoughts and ways are unimaginably higher than ours. And He is love. Because we are secure in His love, we sometimes lose sight of how holy and awe-inspiring God is. Not that we can really comprehend how holy and awe-inspiring He is! But as much as our finite little minds can grasp . . . we forget even that limited understanding of God's majesty.

Just as we often feel both humbled and exhilarated by the mountains, it is fitting to be humbled and exhilarated in God's presence. We cannot comprehend His mind or His thoughts, and yet He kindly invites us to draw near. As it says in Micah 6:8, "He has shown you, O mortal, what is good. And what does the LORD require of you? To act justly and to love mercy and to walk humbly with your God."

Dear Father, You are my Creator, my Redeemer, and my Lord. I yield to You, and I worship You. Thank You for Your kindness. Please shepherd me through this day.

MOUNTAINSIDE PRAYER

After he had dismissed them, he went up on a mountainside by himself to pray.

MATTHEW 14:23

Do you ever feel like your day is just too hectic to squeeze in time alone with God? We all have days like that, don't we? It turns out that even Jesus occasionally had to work at it to find time alone with His Father. For instance, Matthew 14 opens with the account of why John the Baptist was beheaded. Then Jesus fed the five thousand, and later He walked on water. Those are big events, and it's easy to miss what Jesus did in between. He went looking for solitude in order to pray—twice. The first time is in verse 13, when He had just heard about John's death. However, the crowds heard that He had taken a boat to a solitary place, and they followed Him on foot.

Though most of us don't have crowds following us around, we do run into obstacles to our time alone with God. Texts, e-mails, and phone calls can reach us anywhere. Kids who usually can't be pried away from a screen suddenly need us *right now*. Our own minds light up like pinball machines, pinging from one concern to the next. How we need the quiet!

So how did Jesus respond when He saw the crowd waiting for Him on shore? "He had compassion on them and healed their sick" (v. 14), and then He fed them all. He might have been tired and disappointed; He may have been aching with grief for John the Baptist. But He was tenderhearted toward the people who needed Him.

Then He tried again. He sent the disciples ahead on the boat, and He dismissed the crowd. Then, finally, He had time by Himself on the mountainside to pray.

If Jesus, who is one with the Father (John 10:30), sought time alone with the Father, how much more do we need it! We may have to try and try again. That's okay. God is still there, waiting to welcome us.

Dear Lord, thank You for all that we learn about You from Scripture. Please help me to respond with compassion when I am needed at inconvenient times. Help me to keep trying so that I find my time with You.

CAMPING

Let us consider how we may spur one another on toward love and good
deeds, not giving up meeting together . . . but encouraging one another.

HEBREWS 10:24–25

Part of the fun of camping or backpacking is sharing the adventure with our companions: the misery of the grueling hike to the campsite, the mosquitoes that will not quit, the mysterious noise in the middle of the night that turns out to be just porcupines, not bears. All those not-too-fun moments become stories to laugh about later. Of course some moments truly *are* enjoyable—a breathtaking view, butterflies weaving through wildflowers, a swim in a shockingly cold lake, fresh-caught fish, s'mores around the campfire. And there are shared projects: working together to put up the tent, to cook meals outdoors, to secure the food out of reach of those nosy bears, to break camp and clean up. For anyone who enjoys the outdoors, it can be a great bonding experience.

Sometimes the church draws together in a similar way. There are important jobs we've been given to do: to be Christ's witnesses and to care for widows and orphans, for instance. We often have fun together, whether it's at a barbecue, a day at a water park, a ski retreat, or just a gathering of friends over coffee. Then of course there are necessary, practical tasks, such as helping with church cleanup days and giving money to pay staff and keep the lights on. Being the church means collaborating with other believers. Maybe it can also be an adventure that brings us together.

Father, thank You for all Your good gifts, including the
beautiful outdoors, our fellow believers, and the work
You have for us to do. Help us to work together with
joyful hearts, knowing that this pleases You.

FLAX FLOWERS

"See how the flowers of the field grow. They do not labor or spin. Yet I tell you that not even Solomon in all his splendor was dressed like one of these. If that is how God clothes the grass of the field, which is here today and tomorrow is thrown into the fire, will he not much more clothe you—you of little faith? . . . Therefore do not worry about tomorrow, for tomorrow will worry about itself. Each day has enough trouble of its own."

MATTHEW 6:28–30, 34

Wildflowers are a gift, blooming without coaxing or cultivation. And what could be more extravagant than a flower that blooms for only one day? Although a flax plant may produce flowers all summer long, each bloom lasts for just one day. Early in the morning, the teardrop-shaped bud unfurls into a cylinder, and from there into a sort of pinwheel, its five petals tucked one beneath the next with geometric precision, forming a pale blue cup. As the morning sun reaches it, the petals open fully. Sometimes the flower turns toward the sun, petals spread nearly flat into a disc. By evening it droops, looking soft and fragile. The next morning, other buds are still suspended like beads from the curving gray-green stem, but the petals of yesterday's bloom lie wrinkled and scattered at the base of the plant. Later there will be seed pods like little globe-shaped hanging lanterns, each containing five dark, smooth seeds. But the beauty of the flower is given to just one day.

Sometimes one day is all we are given too. In the Lord's Prayer, Jesus says, "Give us *today* our *daily* bread" (Matthew 6:11). When God sent manna in the desert for the Israelites, it lasted for only one day, except for what fell the day before the Sabbath. If the people wanted to eat, they had to gather it six days a week. Of course there are seasons for planning, but in some key areas of life, *daily* is the necessary rhythm. Eating. Sleeping. Praying.

Whatever we do, whether we are receiving a gift from God or following as He leads, today is the time.

Thank You, Lord, for today. I turn my face to You to receive love, life, and guidance, and to pour back praise and obedience. How do You want my life to bloom today?

TAMARACKS

There is a time for everything, and a season for every activity under the heavens:
a time to be born and a time to die, a time to plant and a time to uproot.

ECCLESIASTES 3:1–2

Autumn in the western mountains can look a bit drab compared to the flaming colors of New England or the carefully chosen trees in our own neighborhoods. Most of the wildflowers are gone, and grasses have turned brown. In some areas, vine maple provides one of the few flashes of brilliant orange. Aspen leaves do turn a lovely gold color, and their soft rustling becomes a clattering, as though the trees themselves shiver.

The coniferous trees stand tall and dark on the ridges and hillsides—with one exception. The needles of the western larch, often called the tamarack, turn a lovely pale flame orange. Scattered among the evergreen species, they dapple the landscape with fall.

Tourists often ask, "What is killing all those trees?" But this is not the deep rust color of a dead evergreen. It is the glowing autumn coat of a deciduous conifer. During the winter, the needles will fall. Come spring, these same trees will glow with the soft green of new needles.

Our lives have seasons as well, and cycles of loss and regrowth. Sometimes we mistakenly assume that everyone moves through these seasons in the same pattern. There can be joy and solace in sharing life's stages and challenges with our friends. But what happens when events don't conform to the timeline we expect?

The tamarack reminds us that our Creator does not design identical carbon copies. He is extravagant in the variety and nuance in His creation. When we seek Him—and sometimes even when we don't—He guides each of us through the seasons in the way that we need to go, providing what we need for the journey.

Remember that although the tamarack may not be a typical conifer, its unusual color is the very quality that makes it so beautiful and enlivens the autumn landscape.

Dear Father, thank You that You are a Creator of surprising variety and inventiveness. You know me better than I know myself—and You know what I need better than I do. Please help me to recognize Your provision for me in this season and to receive it gratefully, even if it's not what I had expected.

ON THE MOUNTAINTOP

"The Advocate, the Holy Spirit, whom the Father will send in my name, will teach you all things and will remind you of everything I have said to you."

JOHN 14:26

As we ascend a mountain, we can't see the whole peak. Whether we're driving, hiking, or hanging off a sheer rock face, all that we can see is the stretch immediately in front of us. And that's enough. By completing the stretch in front of us and continuing on to the next, we'll get all the way to the top and down the other side, if that's where we're headed!

There may be stunning views of the surrounding countryside from the top, but the mountain we're standing on? Although we are experiencing it firsthand, we can't see the totality of it while we're right on top of it. To take it all in, to see the shape and size of it and how it dominates the landscape, we get a better perspective from the valley below or the plains in the distance. There, after the blisters and bruises of the ascent (or the broken bones of our descent!) have healed, we are amazed that we were *on* that peak!

Similarly, when we have a spiritual "mountaintop experience," we can only guess just how big it will loom in the landscape of our lives. Maybe it's a mission trip, summer camp, retreat, or conference, a spiritual victory we had prayed about for years, or any season of particularly sweet closeness to Him. How will God use this treasured time in the days or years to come?

While we're on the mountaintop, we can't know, and we don't need to worry about it. That's the time to just soak it up. Later, when we are back on the flatlands or in the valleys, we will better understand the shape of that time. The exhilaration will have melted away, and the work that the Holy Spirit has been doing in us will become clear.

Dear Lord, thank You for Your guidance both on the mountaintop and in the valleys—and everywhere else You lead me! Thank You that Your Holy Spirit is always here to comfort me, teach me, and remind me of what You have said. Help me to be quick to listen and obey.

OUTDOOR TECH

*"I will ask the Father, and he will give you another advocate
to help you and be with you forever—the Spirit of truth."*

As beautiful as they are, the mountains can be treacherous terrain. When people rely too much on apps and technology, it can lead to mishaps that range from humorously inconvenient to downright tragic. Drivers who are overconfident in their four-wheel-drive SUVs may slide off icy roads into the ditch while more careful drivers with less impressive vehicles trundle safely on their way. Hikers using online information have been known to lose the trail or get stranded in winter storms. Driving apps have taken people miles out of the way on bad roads. Visitors from out of town following GPS directions get stuck in heavy snow on roads no local resident would have taken at that time of year. There's no substitute for local, on-the-ground knowledge. Even the wisest people can get caught by a freak storm or car trouble, but often it's our own pride that gets in the way of asking for directions . . . or help or advice.

For just about every endeavor, there are apps, podcasts, Pinterest boards, and YouTube videos. In our high-tech, media-saturated society, it's easy to think, *I got this.*

So . . . how often do we stop to pray?

Jesus promised us the most fantastic resource imaginable—the Holy Spirit. He is our Counselor, Comforter, Helper, Guide, and Advocate. He is the Spirit of truth. He is here to remind us what Jesus taught. He transforms us and He loves us. We can turn to Him anytime because He is with us and in us.

Does that mean we shouldn't make careful preparation to the best of our ability? Of course not! But how amazing it is that at every step along the way, even when we're digging out from under a deep snowdrift of unexpected problems, the Holy Spirit is here with God's power to guide us, teach us, supply us, comfort us, and love us.

No app is going to give you all that.

O Lord, amid all the great gadgets and tech that I enjoy, help me to remember that You are my source of life and deepest wisdom. Thank You for the tender, vital work the Holy Spirit does in me. I yield to You!

HAWKS AND JAYS

Confess your sins to each other and pray for each other so that you may
be healed. The prayer of a righteous person is powerful and effective.

JAMES 5:16

In the mountains, as in most wild places, predators stalk their prey. The Cooper's hawk, for instance, will eat smaller, medium-sized birds. Cooper's hawks are fierce-looking raptors, with impressive talons and beaks. A single bird such as a jay or a flicker or a mourning dove—especially a young one—seems like it would be easy pickings for the larger bird. But jays are smarter than that. If a Cooper's hawk starts skulking around, hoping to snag a tender young fledgling, the smaller birds don't scatter in alarm. Rather, they *give* the alarm, shrieking at the hawk with raucous voices. They harass it relentlessly. Eventually, the hawk may leave, looking for more vulnerable prey.

We might learn something from those jays. First Peter 5 tells us that our enemy the devil is also "looking for someone to devour" (v. 8). Sometimes as Christians, we are afraid to admit that we're in spiritual trouble. It feels less risky to put on our Sunday faces and pretend that everything is fine. But how can our brothers and sisters—our spiritual "nest mates"—help us if they don't know we need it? Fellowship with trusted believers can offer a lifeline of prayer and encouragement. Together we can make noise in prayer and praise, fighting together against temptation and spiritual attacks.

Thankfully, it is not all up to us. In Matthew 18:20, Jesus said, "Where two or three gather in my name, there am I with them." God has promised both to hear us and to be with us.

O Lord, thank You for entrusting us to one another as Your children. Help me to protect and defend and encourage my vulnerable "nest mates." Thank You that You are with us and that You hear our prayers.

COUNTLESS SUNSETS

Let us run with perseverance the race marked out for us,
fixing our eyes on Jesus, the pioneer and perfecter of faith.

HEBREWS 12:1–2

Sunset in the mountains can take a thousand different forms. On a stormy day, clouds may blanket the peaks from view entirely. On a clearer evening, alpenglow can light up the western snow-covered slopes after lower elevations are already in shadow. For people east of the mountains, the looming shapes often become deep purple silhouettes against the golds, pinks, and oranges of sunset. As the sun drops, those brilliant pink clouds fade to purple and then to gray. Sometimes on a cloudy day, mountains in the distance may be under clear skies, bold against a brilliant strip of golden sky along the horizon. We may have our favorite colors, but who's to say one sunset is better than another? Each day's weather is different, and there is no competition.

As we journey through our lives, it's the same. Each of us is an individual, and each of us enjoys and endures unique "weather"—our families and circumstances, our own strengths and weaknesses, various blessings and losses, triumphs and setbacks, hopes and regrets. How then could any two of us have an identical race?

It's all too easy to compare and judge ourselves—and others—as though there's one standard course with identical benchmarks. But our Lord is far too creative for that. When He made human beings in His image, He breathed into us infinite possibilities. Though our potential is all too often stunted and twisted by sin and sorrow, His grace abounds even more. Just as no two sunsets are the same, each person's journey can be brilliant and one of a kind as well. We are not called to be like everyone else, but rather to follow God faithfully on the course He has marked out for each of us.

O Lord, please forgive me for the times I have measured myself against someone else's life. Thank You that You are with me through my life journey. Please help me to run the race with endurance and finish well.

SNOWSTORMS

"Have you entered the storehouses of the snow or seen the storehouses of the hail, which I reserve for times of trouble, for days of war and battle?"

JOB 38:22–23

If you've ever driven over a mountain pass in a snowstorm, you may feel like you *have* seen God's storehouses of snow and hail! When a storm rolls in, clouds envelop the peaks. Snow flies thick toward your windshield, and tall evergreens are soon cloaked in white. While the kids in the backseat may be enchanted by a landscape that looks like Christmas, the adult behind the wheel often has white knuckles! The roads get slick, and it can be nearly impossible to tell where the pavement ends and the soft shoulder begins. Some drivers pull over into designated areas to put chains on their tires. Snowplows and gravel trucks are a welcome sight, working to improve the driving conditions.

Storms of all kinds are painful reminders of just how powerless we can be. How do we respond? How do we approach the Lord in those tumultuous seasons? Poor Job was hit with so much: the deaths of his children, the loss of material wealth and comfort, and the ruining of his physical health. When he questioned God, the Lord's response was to remind him at length exactly who He was, and who Job was not. Snow was one in a long list of things that God created, understands, and has power over. Though He never explained any purpose for Job's suffering, Job was chastened and replied, "Surely I spoke of things I did not understand, things too wonderful for me to know" (Job 42:3). How often do we respond to God with that kind of trust and humility in the storm?

O my Creator, thank You for snow. Thank You for the beauty and infinite variety of those tiny flakes. Thank You that You are in control even during the storms of life—blizzards and every other kind! I trust You to bring me through them, for Your love, power, and wisdom are far beyond my understanding.

STONES OF REMEMBRANCE

Joshua set up at Gilgal the twelve stones they had taken out of the Jordan. He said
to the Israelites, "In the future when your descendants ask their parents, 'What
do these stones mean?' tell them, 'Israel crossed the Jordan on dry ground.' For
the LORD your God dried up the Jordan before you until you had crossed over. . . .
He did this so that all the peoples of the earth might know that the hand of the
LORD is powerful and so that you might always fear the LORD your God."

JOSHUA 4:20–24

Sometimes in the mountains when you're out hiking along a trail, or perhaps driving on a dirt road, you may come upon a little stack of stones. What are they for? Sometimes, a pile of rocks is used in place of a fencepost where there are no trees. Similarly, surveyors may arrange them around a boundary marker or other reference point to hold it in place. In certain places a stack of rocks marks a trail, but others are just an artful lark to add whimsy to the path. Some of these look like little people; others are clearly challenges to the law of gravity!

Many times in the Old Testament, the Lord instructed people to gather stones but with a far more serious, deliberate purpose. Rather than lighthearted diversions, these rock piles were reminders of God's power and faithfulness to His chosen people and a teaching tool for passing that knowledge to the next generation.

What sort of remembrance have you built to remind you of God's deliverance in your own life? Perhaps a ring you wear, words featured in your home, or a family tradition you keep? There are countless ways to honor God's goodness in our lives.

Thank You, Father, for the places in my life where You parted deep waters for me and led me through safely on dry ground. I remember Your power and faithfulness to me. Help me to share that story with others who need to hear it, especially within my own family.

WILDFIRE'S AFTERMATH

The Lord is good to those whose hope is in him. . . . For no one is cast off by the Lord forever. Though he brings grief, he will show compassion, so great is his unfailing love.

LAMENTATIONS 3:25, 31–32

After a wildfire, the land may look completely barren. Firefighters often call an area where all the vegetation was consumed a "Nuke Zone." A few of the larger trees might still be standing, blackened snags, but the grasses, brush, small trees, and downed logs on the forest floor may be totally burnt up. The ash left behind is often several inches deep. Even the soil can be scorched.

However, all is not dead. Sometimes while the area is still smoking, deer wander through, occasionally licking the burnt snags for minerals. The lodgepole pine cones that were tightly sealed have been opened by the high temperatures of the fire, their seeds scattered. If the fire occurs early in the summer, there may be new growth by fall: a few shoots of grass, a flower here and there. By the next spring, the area may be carpeted with wildflowers. A couple of years later, new brush provides lush food for deer and elk. The population of mice often spikes, followed by an increase in coyotes and hawks the following year. As insects move into the snags, woodpeckers drill holes into the wood, providing homes for other birds and squirrels. New trees push their way up through the soil. The forest is not the same; fire has changed the character of the area. But healing and life continue.

Sometimes our lives can feel like a Nuke Zone as well. Perhaps we have suffered the death of a loved one or gone through a divorce. Maybe we lost our job or have been diagnosed with a life-changing disease. Our days feel ashy and lifeless. We may even feel abandoned by God. However, as time goes by, new life peeks through the devastation. We begin to sense God's compassion and love. A Bible passage may take on new meaning and joy because we have new understanding born out of the fire. In time, abundance returns. Our lives may not be the same as they were before, but healing and life continue.

Lord, thank You for Your Word, for all that it shows us about You. Thank You for Your compassion and unfailing love.

LANDMARK

Trust in the Lord with all your heart and lean not on your own understanding;
in all your ways submit to him, and he will make your paths straight.

PROVERBS 3:5–6

In some neighborhoods, it's easy to lose your sense of direction. The houses all look alike, the landscaping is more or less the same, and there are no distinctive landmarks. In a mountain town, it's a different story. It's never difficult to figure out what direction you're facing. If you can see the mountain, you can orient yourself. There will be other landmarks, but none so useful from just about any vantage point. Rivers and highways disappear from view within a few blocks. Even the tallest trees, grandest buildings, and biggest billboards sink out of sight by the time you've gone about a mile. But a nearby mountain can be glimpsed from almost anywhere; at most all you have to do is walk a short distance or turn around to spot it.

What orients us in our day-to-day life? Do we have an overwhelming landmark? Or just the confusion of competing claims on our focus? Some signposts are quite useful in specific situations: the best practices of a particular profession; the guidelines of a specific discipline; the code of conduct of our company; even the etiquette of everyday life. But each of these covers just a small arena compared with the Bible. The principles revealed in Scripture give guidance for all of life, and they go deeper, too, addressing not just our actions or even our intentions, but our very hearts. The Bible holds up a mirror for us. "Anyone who listens to the word but does not do what it says is like someone who looks at his face in a mirror and, after looking at himself, goes away and immediately forgets what he looks like. But whoever looks intently into the perfect law that gives freedom, and continues in it—not forgetting what they have heard, but doing it—they will be blessed in what they do" (James 1:23–25).

Best of all, the Bible reveals who God is and how much He loves us. What could be a better guide than that?

Father, thank You for Your Word. Please forgive me for being distracted by other voices. Help me to orient myself to You.

SURVIVING WINTER

There are different kinds of gifts, but the same Spirit distributes them. There are different kinds of service, but the same Lord. There are different kinds of working, but in all of them and in everyone it is the same God at work.

1 CORINTHIANS 12:4—6

In the winter, snow-capped peaks rise majestically over the wintry landscape, but all sorts of creatures face a challenge in surviving until spring. Wolves, coyotes, and mountain lions hunt or scavenge all winter. Deer and elk must forage for food. Most bears fatten up and hibernate, their heartbeat and metabolism slowing so that their reserves of body fat supply sustenance through the colder months. Some bats do the same, roosting together in caves. Squirrels stay awake throughout the winter, eating food they have stockpiled in a den or nest. So do pikas, a member of the rabbit family that lives in the rocks in high elevations. Each creature's coping mechanisms for the harsh weather are suited to its strengths and weaknesses.

God is so creative, isn't He? What care He has put into making each animal a unique creation! As Jesus said in Matthew 10:29, "Are not two sparrows sold for a penny? Yet not one of them will fall to the ground outside your Father's care."

God extends His creativity to us as well. The apostle Paul wrote about this at length in 1 Corinthians 12, comparing the church to a physical body. A whole and healthy body, functioning as God envisions, requires variety. "If the whole body were an eye, where would the sense of hearing be? If the whole body were an ear, where would the sense of smell be? But in fact God has placed the parts in the body, every one of them, just as he wanted them to be. If they were all one part, where would the body be? As it is, there are many parts, but one body" (vv. 17–20).

Our differences are not always a cause for concern or conflict. It takes all of us, using our gifts in various ways, to make His church whole and healthy. We can celebrate that!

Dear Father, thank You for the variety in Your creation and in Your church. Please guide me in how You want me to use the particular gifts You have given me.

HEARTS

For the eyes of the LORD range throughout the earth to
strengthen those whose hearts are fully committed to him.

2 CHRONICLES 16:9

Come with me up on the mountain! Look out over the landscape. What do you see? Ridge after ridge of tree-covered land? Perhaps a city in the distance? Maybe boats on a nearby lake or hikers coming up the trail? Whatever sights we may scan from the peak, they are not likely to include a detailed look at people far away. Even with powerful binoculars, we cannot get a close look.

How different that is from the way God sees us! He not only perceives us clearly, He can see so much more than what's on the outside. In 1 Samuel 16, God sent Samuel to Jesse's house to anoint one of his sons as king over Israel. Samuel thought the first son looked like a good candidate, but God told him, "The LORD does not look at the things people look at. People look at the outward appearance, but the LORD looks at the heart" (v. 7). It turned out that God wanted the youngest brother, David, to be the next king of Israel. He was a man after God's own heart (Acts 13:22). No wonder he was the man God had in mind! David later wrote in Psalm 139, "Search me, God, and know my heart; test me and know my anxious thoughts. See if there is any offensive way in me, and lead me in the way everlasting" (vv. 23–24). David surely knew that God did not need an invitation to know his heart and his thoughts, and yet he welcomed God's scrutiny and guidance.

What about us? How are our hearts? Are they open to the God who loves us? Or have we allowed the difficulties of life to harden our hearts? In Ezekiel 36:26, God told the Israelites, "I will give you a new heart and put a new spirit in you; I will remove from you your heart of stone and give you a heart of flesh." Now that is a beautiful promise. Surely He can renew our hearts as well!

O Lord, I open my heart to You today. Search me, and see what needs to be changed. Guide me and make me into a person after Your own heart.

EROSION AND ERUPTIONS

"My sheep listen to my voice; I know them, and they follow me. I give them eternal life, and they shall never perish; no one will snatch them out of my hand. My Father, who has given them to me, is greater than all; no one can snatch them out of my Father's hand. I and the Father are one."

JOHN 10:27–30

Often, change comes gradually, like the erosion of a creek bank year after year, or the infinitesimal wearing of the wind on a granite cliff face. Trees grow taller year by year, and ravines are carved a bit deeper. But the broader landscape does not change. Day passes after day, one season giving way to another, often fast-paced, but with no major upheaval. The kids grow older and taller year by year. The faces in our churches and neighborhoods are mostly constant. We struggle with some things—maybe our child's teacher is not who we had hoped for, or we're at odds with a family member or a neighbor. But the patterns are not radically different year after year.

Then there are seasons when change feels more like Mount St. Helens' erupting. Do you remember what happened that day? One side of the mountain was blown out. Steaming hot ash boiled into the sky. The shock wave knocked down miles upon miles of forest. A river of mud and ash obliterated a wide swath of terrain. Have you been there in your own life? A loved one passes away unexpectedly. We receive a terrifying medical diagnosis. Our marriage ends. Best friends move halfway across the country. A disagreement that seemed minor to us severs a close relationship. Our pastor retires, and within months our church becomes unrecognizable. And in some seasons, it's not just one change, but one after another.

What never changes is that Jesus is our Shepherd. When our world lurches off-kilter, we may momentarily forget that we are in Jesus' hand, in the Father's hand. But we are. No matter how strong the shock wave of change feels, nothing can snatch us out of His hand.

Dear Father, thank You that You hold me securely in Your hand. I surrender my fears to You. Help me to hear Your voice every day, especially during times of disorienting change.

WILDLIFE

In their hearts humans plan their course, but the LORD establishes their steps.

PROVERBS 16:9

No matter how thoroughly we plan, it's impossible to know what kind of wildlife we might see in the mountains. Will it be deer standing cautiously at the edge of a meadow, watching us? A fox or coyote silently weaving among the trees? A covey of quail, scurrying along, then pausing, then scurrying some more, and finally taking flight at our approach? A moose, picking her way across a hillside on long legs? A hawk diving for prey? A bear pausing to size us up from a distance?

For most of us, these sorts of encounters are delightful serendipity. They become far more unlikely if we race along the trail, focused only on covering a certain number of miles by lunchtime or before dark. What quiet treasure waits to be noticed, just a stone's throw off the trail? A rabbit foraging in the brush early in the morning? Ladybugs swarming on a late summer afternoon? Pronghorns coming down to a lake to drink at sunset? Raccoons, quite bold? Bats, flying in erratic swoops as they feed on bugs in the twilight? An otter swimming in a river as darkness falls?

So it is with everyday life. We plan and strategize and schedule. We download apps and design elaborate bullet journals. But let's face it: the days will inevitably unfold with some surprises, with crises and headaches and delays. If we clutch our plans too tightly, we miss the delightful possibilities waiting for us if we will just raise our eyes from our to-do list. The friend we haven't talked to in a while who'd love to hear from us. The child who feels unnoticed in a group of adults, but whose smile will light up the room if we talk to her. The widow we've always liked who has no family nearby and grows lonely. They're not far off the beaten path of our routine. Who is God inviting us to notice today?

O Lord, I yield my day and all my plans to You. Please help me to work diligently at them—and to be ready to lay them aside when You nudge me to take a detour. I am all Yours.

ALPENGLOW

Every good and perfect gift is from above, coming down from the
Father of the heavenly lights, who does not change like shifting shadows.

JAMES 1:17

Sometimes on a clear day, just before the sun rises, snowy mountain peaks are bathed in soft glowing tones of pink, purple, or gold. This phenomenon (which can also happen in the evening just after sunset) is called alpenglow. The slopes light up like beacons of the coming day while the observer still stands in the cold predawn shade.

Have you ever seen signs of God's grace glowing in the distance while your own circumstances were shrouded in gloom? In this world, the shadows do shift, often falling across our lives, bringing darkness and cold. During difficult seasons, it can seem like the Lord is very far away from us. Although we've been told that He is with us even in the darkest valley, we can't always sense His presence. But sometimes, before we feel the warmth of God's healing on our own faces and shoulders, in our own hearts and minds, we can see it in someone else's situation. The glory of God's grace nearby is a harbinger that He will shine His face on us as well. We are promised in 1 John 3:2 that "we shall be like him, for we shall see him as he is." And it says in 1 Corinthians 13 that we shall know Him fully, even as we are fully known (v. 12). So even when we don't *feel* His love and grace, we know that in time, we will become fully aware of those gifts He is pouring out over us. And that is a hope brighter than any sunrise alpenglow.

O Lord, thank You that You have promised to be with me, no matter how dark my road is—even in the valley of the shadow of death! Draw my attention to those signs of Your glory and Your approach. I rejoice in the light You bring to each new day and the good gifts You give me.

SUMMER THUNDERSTORMS

Whoever dwells in the shelter of the Most High will rest in the shadow of the Almighty.
I will say of the LORD, "He is my refuge and my fortress, my God, in whom I trust."

PSALM 91:1–2

Hiking in the summertime brings so much joy: going outdoors, breathing fresh air, leaving stale or chaotic surroundings behind. In the mountains, we breathe deeply and let our eyes roam over beautiful countryside and distant vistas. We pass among trees and wildflowers; we catch glimpses of birds, deer, and other wildlife. Maybe we follow the course of a stream or the shore of a high mountain lake.

Sometimes as the path climbs higher, that wide-open atmosphere changes unexpectedly. Clouds darken the day. The wind that had been sighing softly among the trees picks up speed, thrashing through the branches.

At this point, a wise and experienced hiker—or a cautious one—heads for shelter, perhaps back to the car or the cabin. A storm is coming, with rain and the danger of lightning. Wild weather can be exhilarating, but less experienced hikers are fortunate if they have someone to warn them and guide them to safety.

Sometimes this happens in everyday life, too. We're on a path that seems so pleasant to us. We're breathing deeply, enjoying our surroundings, our activities, our companions. They may offer beauty or excitement, solace or belonging. And then . . . spiritual unease clouds our way. The Holy Spirit tugs at us, signaling our spirit that all is not well, that we are in danger. What started out so enjoyably has become a walk that may harm us spiritually. When this happens, we need to ask ourselves, *Is there another route open to us, leading to a place of refuge?* When the storm clouds gather, we are wise to seek shelter.

O Lord, thank You that You watch over me, that You see the path before me and know what lies ahead. Help me to be aware of Your guidance and quick to follow Your lead.

BLANKETS OF SNOW

"Though your sins are like scarlet, they shall be as white as snow."

ISAIAH 1:18

Ah, snow-capped peaks. The white looks so pristine, especially when it's gleaming against a blue sky. What could be purer than snow? Intricate, delicate, six-sided crystals of ice. For all their individual complexity, when snowflakes pile up, they all blend together. Then snow has a way of covering ugliness. A fresh snowfall of several inches not only blankets everything in white, it muffles shapes and sounds, and it softens harsh edges. It can be hard to guess what's under those white mounds! Is it a bush or a doghouse? A grill or a garbage can? A well-tended lawn or a trash-strewn weed patch? A child's toy or one of Dad's tools? Is that your car in the crowded parking lot, or one that looks just like it? A car alongside the road, or just a big berm of snow thrown there by the plow? Sometimes a familiar place becomes practically unrecognizable!

Of course, in most parts of the world, this transformation is temporary. A light snowfall may melt off in a matter of hours. Others may last for days, weeks, or even months up in the mountains. Snowplows, car tires, and human feet make paths through the snow. Sunshine, warm air, rain, and wind all take their toll. Those mysterious piles of snow shrivel and reveal what's underneath. Eventually, pine needles, grass, and bare ground start to emerge. The snow melts away—often leaving a muddy mess!

When the Lord says our sins shall be white as snow, He's not talking about this temporary hiding, merely leaving our sins there and covering them up. God remembers our sins no more. In fact, Psalm 51:7 says that when He washes us, we will be whiter than snow! That's hard to imagine, isn't it? Yet "if we confess our sins, he is faithful and just and will forgive us our sins and purify us from all unrighteousness" (1 John 1:9).

We are forgiven completely.

O Lord, I confess my sins to You, and I leave them behind. Thank You for cleansing me. Thank You for snow and for the beauty of Your Word.

THE BIG PICTURE

I lift up my eyes to the mountains—where does my help come from?
My help comes from the LORD, the Maker of heaven and earth.

PSALM 121:1–2

We spend a lot of time focusing on what's right in front of us—meals to prepare, children to feed, errands to run, calendars to manage—not to mention our phones! Sometimes we charge right through a day and hardly stop to catch our breath.

The world is full of advice and slogans telling us our lives are what we make of them, that it is all up to us, that if we use the right products and download the smartest apps and implement best practices, we can crush this life. (*Crush*: How has a word meaning to destroy become a synonym for achievement?)

Ah, but when we lift our eyes, the big picture emerges. The long view comes into focus. Our gaze rests on the mountains, on the beauty and majesty of something far beyond our control. The Lord created heaven and earth, including these soaring peaks that catch our eyes and pull us out of ourselves. They loom over the landscape season after season, often shining white in the sun, in the evening at times purple-black against a blazing sunset, and sometimes concealed in storm clouds. The mountains remind us that we are one small aspect of God's creation. And yet we are so dear to His heart that He knows us and He helps us, even to the point of sacrificing His Son to save us. Our God is so good to us. Praise His name!

O Lord my Creator, thank You for being my help. Help me to look up frequently, to see the mountains and remember who I am: just one person in Your beautiful creation and yet Your beloved and valued child.

HOME

The Lord is my rock, my fortress and my deliverer; my God is my rock, in
whom I take refuge, my shield and the horn of my salvation, my stronghold.

PSALM 18:2

What comes to mind when you imagine a home in the mountains? Maybe you picture a rustic log cabin with a wood stove and a spring out back for water. Or perhaps something more impressive, a grand lodge with soaring ceilings, huge fireplaces, big, chunky furniture, and wool throw blankets. Or perhaps your mind jumps to Europe, to a castle perched on a rocky outcropping so that it seems to grow out of the sheer stone cliffs like a fairy-tale palace. Or maybe you already live there, and you see it every day!

The Bible describes God Himself as our refuge and fortress. He is our dwelling place, our home. In Him we live and move and have our being. Surely there is no more secure place to be. And what a privilege to be invited to make our life in Him!

Scripture also offers us hope about our home in the world to come. Jesus told His disciples, "My Father's house has many rooms; if that were not so, would I have told you that I am going there to prepare a place for you? And if I go and prepare a place for you, I will come back and take you to be with me that you also may be where I am" (John 14:2–3). Earthbound as we are, we cannot really know what that place is like. But we can trust our Lord that it will be all that we desire and more.

O Lord, thank You for the ways that You have provided a home
for me, both physically and spiritually. Help me to nestle
in at Your hearthside, secure in Your love and strength.

MOONLIGHT ON SNOW

When I consider your heavens, the work of your fingers, the moon and the stars, which you have set in place, what is mankind that you are mindful of them, human beings that you care for them?

PSALM 8:3–4

Have you ever seen snow-covered mountains on a clear night under a full moon? They reflect the moonlight so well that they practically glow. Although it's normal to see the peaks during daylight, to see them so visibly at night is startling and strange but in a nice way, like running into an old friend when you haven't seen her in a while and weren't expecting her.

If you can get away from the lights of town, moonlight and snow are a dazzling combination. The shadows are sharp, and it's amazing how well you can see.

Genesis describes the creation of the moon on the fourth day. "Let there be lights in the vault of the sky to separate the day from the night, and let them serve as signs to mark sacred times, and days and years, and let them be lights in the vault of the sky to give light on the earth" (Genesis 1:14–15). When God reflected on what He had made that day, He said that it was good. And it is good! How ingenious of God to design and create the solar system! He planned the complex pattern of seasons and weather that come together in moonlight and snow. It is a lavish gift, and He is worthy of our praise!

Dear Father God, my brilliant Creator, thank You for creating the order and splendor of our solar system. The moon and the snow are each lovely on their own—and together, they are stunning. Thank You for designing such beauty and sharing it with us.

MOUNT RUSHMORE

*Yet you, LORD, are our Father. We are the clay, you
are the potter; we are all the work of your hand.*

ISAIAH 64:8

People like to leave their mark, don't they? All around the world, you can find
statues, monuments, and towers. Some were built to honor someone or something greatly admired. Others were built to gratify someone's ego or soothe their
grief. In South Dakota, the Mount Rushmore National Memorial was originally
conceived as a way to promote tourism, but the sculptor envisioned a shrine to
democracy. Blasted and carved out between 1927 and 1941, the sixty-foot faces of
four U.S. presidents look out from the granite cliffs. And it does bring tourists;
nearly three million people visit each year.

God also desires to leave a mark—on us. As it says in Isaiah 64:8, we are the
work of His hand. How reassuring that is! He created us, and He continues to
mold us to become what He planned us to be. That contradicts the wisdom of the
world, doesn't it? We are not the sole designer of our lives. He is our Maker!

The Lord also cautions us in Isaiah 45:9: "Woe to those who quarrel with their
Maker, those who are nothing but potsherds among the potsherds on the ground.
Does the clay say to the potter, 'What are you making?' Does your work say, 'The
potter has no hands'?" As beings created by Him, we need to respect Him!

But Isaiah 64:8 offers us another encouraging insight. In this verse, we are
clay, a soft, malleable material. The potter doesn't need to blast the clay with
dynamite or drill with jackhammers to shape it, as the workers did on Mount
Rushmore. When we offer soft hearts and flexible wills to God, He can fulfill His
purpose for us gently.

O Lord, I bend to Your wishes today. Thank You for creating me. I offer my heart and mind willingly. Please, make me more like You.

LIVING WATER

He makes springs pour water into the ravines; it flows between the mountains.
They give water to all the beasts of the field; the wild donkeys quench their thirst.
The birds of the sky nest by the waters; they sing among the branches. He waters the
mountains from his upper chambers; the land is satisfied by the fruit of his work.

PSALM 104:10–13

Have you ever hiked alongside a mountain stream? The water gurgles and sings as it rushes along. It leaps and dances around boulders and under fallen logs. Vibrant moss carpets the rocks along the banks. Fish linger in shady pools under the overhanging branches. Birds nest in the trees near the water. In the early evening, animals come down to drink. The water is cold and fresh, and even in the tranquil pools, it is always, always moving.

In Jeremiah 2:13, the Lord declares, "My people have committed two sins: They have forsaken me, the spring of living water, and have dug their own cisterns, broken cisterns that cannot hold water." That sounds crazy, doesn't it? Who would do that? Of course, we have all done it from time to time.

The good news is that God is gracious and forgiving. "Jesus stood and said in a loud voice, 'Let anyone who is thirsty come to me and drink. Whoever believes in me, as Scripture has said, rivers of living water will flow from within them.' By this he meant the Spirit, whom those who believed in him were later to receive" (John 7:37–39). This is not stale, brackish water, stagnant and dead. He is the source of life itself, continually fresh and new. How exhilarating is our God!

O Lord, You are the source of all life. Thank You for offering
Yourself to us. Please flow through me today. Refresh
and replenish me, and refresh others through me!

SERVING GOD

But God chose the foolish things of the world to shame the wise; God chose the
weak things of the world to shame the strong. God chose the lowly things of this
world and the despised things . . . so that no one may boast before him.

1 CORINTHIANS 1:27–29

D id you know that dead trees are essential to forest ecosystems? In fact, when
timber is harvested, logging contracts often require that a certain number
of dead trees are left standing on each acre of land. Why? Those snags provide habitat for all kinds of wildlife. Birds, squirrels, honeybees, raccoons, skunks, foxes,
opossums, and even black bears may live in them. Although no longer flourishing
as they once did, those trees still nurture life.

Sometimes, we may feel that our usefulness to God has run its course.
Perhaps we've weathered some upheaval such as a move or a job change. For whatever reason, we find ourselves unable to serve as we did in the past, in ways that are
meaningful to us.

However, God is not limited by our abilities. He has often worked through
people in surprising ways. For example, when there was a terrible drought in Israel,
God didn't send Elijah to a wealthy family with a well-stocked pantry. He sent him
to a widow who was down to her last meal for herself and her son, and He provided
for all three of them until the drought ended. God *decreased* the size of Gideon's
army twice before He sent him to fight the Midianites, saying, "You have too many
men. I cannot deliver Midian into their hands, or Israel would boast against me,
'My own strength has saved me'" (Judges 7:2).

Sometimes God uses the strengths He has given us. Other times, He uses our
weaknesses, so that His power shines through. When we yield to God all that we
are, there's no telling what He might do with us. Isn't that exciting?

O Lord, You created me, and You know me better than I know myself. You also know the needs of all those around me. Whatever You want to do with me, I'm all in.

AVALANCHE

"Therefore everyone who hears these words of mine and puts them into practice is like a wise man who built his house on the rock. The rain came down, the streams rose, and the winds blew and beat against that house; yet it did not fall, because it had its foundation on the rock. But everyone who hears these words of mine and does not put them into practice is like a foolish man who built his house on sand. The rain came down, the streams rose, and the winds blew and beat against that house, and it fell with a great crash."

MATTHEW 7:24–27

Avalanches can happen when heavy snow accumulates on a steep slope on top of older, weaker snow. Eventually the weight of the new snow is too much for the less stable layer beneath, and it gives way. Heavy slabs of snow slide down the slope, eventually tumbling and crashing to a halt farther down the mountain. It's a fearsome side of the snow.

No one would build a house on top of snow in an avalanche zone, but the foolish person Jesus described in Matthew 7 is not so far off from that. He builds on an unstable base. Not surprisingly, during a storm his house falls with a "great crash." We've all seen news footage of homes destroyed in violent weather. How devastating it must be! That's the image of those who hear Jesus' words but do not act on them.

Now, think about how it feels to be inside a solid, well-built house during a wild rainstorm. Snug. Safe. Warm. Dry. We can hear the wind and the rain buffeting the house, and yet we are protected. That's the picture of those who hear Jesus' words and live by them.

Building on a strong foundation may not prevent the storms of life, but it does provide safe shelter.

Thank You, Lord, for speaking so clearly in Scripture. Please help me to act on Your words. I am Yours, and I yield to Your wisdom.

SAFE PASSAGE

*No temptation has overtaken you except what is common to mankind. And God
is faithful; he will not let you be tempted beyond what you can bear. But when
you are tempted, he will also provide a way out so that you can endure it.*

1 CORINTHIANS 10:13

Did you know that in some places, wildlife have their own underpasses? Where busy highways cross migration routes, the deer need safe passage. Collisions between cars and wildlife are often fatal for the animals, and they aren't much fun for the drivers either. Where wildlife crossings are built, the highway is fenced for miles in each direction to funnel animals toward the crossing. They work, too. Motion sensor cameras have captured images of not only deer but also coyotes, raccoons, birds, squirrels, and bobcats using the crossings. That's a lot of animal lives protected!

Like those deer, we can run into danger. For us, it's sin that can leave us in a bad way. James puts it bluntly: "Each person is tempted when they are dragged away by their own evil desire and enticed. Then, after desire has conceived, it gives birth to sin; and sin, when it is full-grown, gives birth to death" (James 1:14–15). Those are pretty stark words, aren't they?

Thankfully, that's not the whole picture. "As a father has compassion on his children, so the Lord has compassion on those who fear him; for he knows how we are formed, he remembers that we are dust" (Psalm 103:13–14). As our Creator, He knows exactly how each of us is inclined to wander and how much we can endure. According to Paul in 1 Corinthians 10:13, God is watching out for us. Where there is temptation, He provides safe passage. God is so good to us!

*Dear Father, thank You for looking out for me! Please help
me to see temptation coming, and show me the way out.*

HEALTHY FORESTS

*And this is my prayer: that your love may abound more and more in knowledge
and depth of insight, so that you may be able to discern what is best and may be
pure and blameless for the day of Christ, filled with the fruit of righteousness
that comes through Jesus Christ—to the glory and praise of God.*

PHILIPPIANS 1:9–11

Have you ever wondered what it takes to keep a forest healthy? Millions of acres are actively managed to help them thrive and to minimize the risk of wildfire.

Forest managers have to know which species grow in their woods. How else can they figure out the best ways to nurture a healthy ecosystem? They walk through it and may designate small plots of land to study. They research the history of the area. Maps, aerial photos, and Google Earth are consulted. Laws and regulations must be followed. The value versus the cost of any plan must be considered. All of this information is compiled to guide them.

What comes of all this? Trees may be thinned, removing some so that the rest will grow better. Brush is often mown or carefully burned to reduce the danger of a catastrophic wildfire. There is always something more that can be done to nurture a healthy forest.

Our spiritual lives need tending too, and God has provided resources for us. We study the Bible, learning how to grow spiritually. We spend time with other believers and pray for one another. We keep an eye on our own spiritual health, and the Holy Spirit gives us insight. Is there sin that needs to be uprooted? Are good activities crowding out even better ways to use our time? Perhaps those need to be thinned. Nurturing our spiritual health is an ongoing process, but it is well worth the effort.

O Lord, You know my heart. You know where I am thriving and where I need help. Please guide me so that I continue growing in You!

AT THE LAKE

He leads me beside quiet waters, he refreshes my soul.

PSALM 23:2–3

When the summer sun bakes our neighborhoods and the heat saps our strength, there's nothing quite as lovely as escaping to a lake in the high country. The temperatures are cooler and the water is so refreshing. There are many ways to unwind: fishing, boating, swimming, or even staying on the shore, enjoying the cool breeze and the scenery. Can't you just feel the tension melting away?

God designed us to need rest, and He created many places in nature that help us find it. He set the example in Scripture by resting on the seventh day of creation. He even told the Israelites to rest. Does it seem strange that the instruction to keep the Sabbath is one of the Ten Commandments, right there among the laws against lying, stealing, and murder? And that's only one of the places it appears. Many regulations about rest, for both the people and the land, are woven throughout His Law in the Old Testament.

Why is this so important to God? One reason is that He wants us to rely on Him for our strength and our refreshment. "In repentance and rest is your salvation, in quietness and trust is your strength" (Isaiah 30:15). When we rest, we are demonstrating our trust in Him, that He will supply all that we need. We can afford to rest because He provides for us.

God is so good and generous to create this beautiful world that we enjoy. Most of us can't get to the lake every day, but we can seek the refreshment of fellowship with Him.

O Lord, please forgive me for my pride, for any times when I have believed that I could not afford to rest. My life belongs to You, and that includes my time and my energy. I yield to You, and I gratefully accept Your gift of rest.

STARGAZING

He counts the number of the stars; He gives names to all of them.
Great is our Lord and abundant in strength; His understanding is infinite.

PSALM 147:4–5 NASB

Moonless summer nights are the perfect time to head out into a high mountain meadow with a group of friends and some blankets to do a little stargazing. It is amazing to watch the Perseid meteor shower in August, or even to just lie back and let yourself fall upward into the brilliance of all those stars. In the quiet, your voices gradually hush as you murmur about what you're seeing: constellations, maybe a plane or satellite gliding along. The Milky Way stretches across the vault of the sky, filmy and luminous. There are so many more stars, in more sizes and colors, than are ever visible in town. They seem to be closer, too.

Long after leaving the meadow and the stars, we're filled up inside, replete with wonder, beauty, joy, and peace. When we understand that we are loved by God, we don't find it alienating to be one person on our one little planet in the bejeweled sky. Instead, we are set free. Not that any of our troubles have miraculously vanished. But our glimpse of the beautiful vastness that spins through the cosmos night after night (whether we notice it or not) reminds us that we're not the center of it all. We didn't set the stars in motion, and it's not up to us to keep them going. We can let God be God while we relax in His love.

O Lord, Your universe is dazzling! The more I learn about
it, the more I am awestruck by Your power and creativity.
Thank You that Your love is as unending as the night sky.

SNAKES AND DOVES

"I am sending you out like sheep among wolves.
Therefore be as shrewd as snakes and as innocent as doves."

MATTHEW 10:16

Deer are prey, so they are very wary. Unless they've been desensitized by a lot of human contact, they tend to spook easily. Dogs in particular will send them bounding away. Dogs are too much like coyotes and wolves, two of the deer's natural predators. Even a small dog, smaller than a housecat, walking on a leash will draw the attention of a herd of deer. They may stop and watch it, their heads moving in unison, their big ears looking like synchronized radar dishes. Deer are not stupid. In their own wild way, they are pretty shrewd.

Are we as watchful as those deer? Do we recognize threats, even small ones, to our well-being? Song of Solomon 2:15 says, "Catch for us the foxes, the little foxes that ruin the vineyards, our vineyards that are in bloom." So many dangers are easier to catch when they are small, whether it is a little sin, a half-truth, the first whiff of corruption, or any tendency in us that is not pleasing to God.

That doesn't mean we need to hunker down and barricade ourselves away. We are in the world, though we are not of it. When Jesus told His disciples to be as shrewd as serpents, He was sending them out among the predators—the wolves—of the world. In place of the word *shrewd*, some other translations use *wise*, *cautious*, or *cunning*. He didn't want His disciples to be easily duped or harmed.

At the same time, He told them to be as innocent as doves. Other translations use *gentle*, *harmless*, or *inoffensive*. Being shrewd or wise does not mean becoming combative, and innocence does not mean going along with anything and everything. It's quite a balance to strike, isn't it?

Dear Lord, thank You for the wisdom I find in in Your Word. Help me to remember Your instructions to Your disciples—and to live by them, not hoodwinked by the dangers around me, but staying true to You.

FINGERS THAWING

I consider that our present sufferings are not worth
comparing with the glory that will be revealed in us.

ROMANS 8:18

Fresh powder beckons, and we flock to the mountains—to ski, snowboard, snowshoe, snowmobile, go tubing, have snowball fights, and even do some winter camping.

Stay out in the cold long enough, though, and eventually those noses, ears, toes, and fingers start to get cold. A hat flies off in a tumble; gloves get a little bit wet. Eventually, it's time to warm up. So we head back to the lodge or the car and strip off some layers, grateful for the warmth and a waiting cup of hot cocoa.

But as blood flow returns to those icy extremities, they begin to tingle. It hurts!

Sometimes spiritual restoration is like that, too. When we wander too far from the life-giving warmth of communion with God, the chill of sin sets in. The lust of the flesh, the lust of the eyes, and the pride of life can keep us out of God's presence longer than we realize.

When we finally do turn back to Him and once again submit to the Holy Spirit, conviction of sin can sting. Our regret for wasted time and missed opportunities may be scalding. If we have lingered in despair or been mired in deep unbelief, the shock of hope and joy melting our malaise can tingle painfully. But just as blood flow returning to our fingers and toes saves us from frostbite, the pains of spiritual restoration are also temporary and ultimately lead us back to warm, abundant life. It's well worth that short-term discomfort to come close to the Lord again!

Thank You, Father, that You always welcome me back into the life-giving warmth of Your presence. Please forgive me if I have been playing with sin, and cleanse me of all that does not please You.

SPRINGTIME

You will go out in joy and be led forth in peace; the mountains and hills will burst into song before you, and all the trees of the field will clap their hands.

ISAIAH 55:12

Springtime may come a bit late to the mountains, but it's a vibrant, busy season nonetheless. If there was snow, the streams rush, swollen with snowmelt, and ravines flood with the seasonal runoff. New growth emerges: grass, wildflowers, leaves, and soft new needles on the evergreens. Bears waken. Caterpillars appear. Squirrels chatter, birds build their nests, and everyone is out looking for food. Soon baby animals will be born, including spotted fawns on spindly legs. Everything is new and noisy and fresh.

It's so fitting that we celebrate Easter in the spring, because Jesus rising from the dead is the ultimate rebirth. When Jesus came riding into Jerusalem on a donkey just days before His crucifixion, a whole crowd of disciples called out, "Blessed is the king who comes in the name of the Lord!" and "Peace in heaven and glory in the highest!" The Pharisees wanted Jesus to silence them, but Jesus replied that if they were quiet, the stones would cry out (Luke 19:37–40). People may forget, but the earth knows who its Lord and Creator is.

What will it be like when the hills and mountains sing and the trees clap their hands? Romans 8 says, "The creation itself will be liberated from its bondage to decay and brought into the freedom and glory of the children of God" (v. 21). If our world is this beautiful now, imagine how stunning it will be when all is restored to God's vision for His creation!

O Lord, my Creator, thank You for making our world so delightful.
I can't wait to see it when You bring it to full redemption!

FIREFIGHTING

*For we are God's handiwork, created in Christ Jesus to do
good works, which God prepared in advance for us to do.*

EPHESIANS 2:10

All across the country, thousands of people work in wildland firefighting every year. Workers stop a wildfire by digging a fire line around it. All plant material is cleared out of the fire line, right down to mineral soil. When the fire reaches the line, it has no fuel and the flames die down.

Sometimes a fire line can be cleared quickly with a bulldozer, but often the terrain requires people using hand tools. Most of the work is done using shovels and specialized pickaxes called Pulaskis. Each swing of the Pulaski or scoop of the shovel clears away potential fuel for the fire. If the conditions are right, firefighters may do a back burn, setting a smaller fire between the fire line and the wildfire. It burns up the fuel, reducing the risk that the fire could blow past the fire line.

Eventually every fire goes out. Sometimes this can be done in a day; other fires continue to burn until the rains come or the snow falls.

Like fighting a wildfire, following God is a process. Sometimes the tasks before us can be overwhelming. However, when we take small steps and work steadily, we can accomplish a lot and know that others are blessed by our efforts.

Sometimes we may need to wait patiently for others to help us, as when firefighters wait for a plane or helicopter to drop fire retardant or water. Other times, we just have to wait for a situation to resolve itself, as when the firefighters build a line quite some distance from the fire and wait for just the right time to start a back burn.

Since we can't see into the future, we rely on the One who not only knows *what* will happen but *when*. The time we spend waiting on the Lord can seem endless, but during the waiting we grow closer to Him.

O Lord, I am so glad that You know the future. Help me to see those good things You have prepared for me to do. Thank You for the adventure of being Your child!

OLD BOOTS

"The grass withers and the flowers fall, but the word of our God endures forever."

ISAIAH 40:8

They sit in a closet or a corner. There may be a bit of mud still clinging to the sole. The leather may be cracked and the tread worn down. Newer, lighter, high-tech footwear has replaced the old hiking boots, yet for nostalgia we keep them. They remind us of the miles we tramped in them. Maybe we wore them when we summited a peak, or perhaps when we walked alongside someone special. So the old boots have stayed even as we discarded other worn-out gear. We might even put them on just to relive the memories.

We may have an old Bible still on the shelf too. The reasons may be similar. Perhaps it reminds us of the first verse we ever memorized. Maybe it was handed down from a loved one or given to us for graduation. We've since set it aside, possibly when we got a new study Bible or switched to an electronic version. But for whatever reason, we still hang on to the old Bible.

Unlike our old boots, the old Bible is just as useful as it ever was—and just as powerful. No recharging is needed to open it and begin reading. Our eyes might be drawn to an underlined passage. What did that verse mean to whoever marked it? Maybe we have notes in the margins from years ago, jottings that remind us of God's faithfulness over time. There is hope, comfort, and healing to be found simply by holding open the Scriptures and seeking the Living Word. God is as near as our fingertips.

O Lord, Your Word is pure and sweeter even than honey.
Thank you for the gift of the Bible! I am so grateful
that You reveal Yourself to us in its pages.

TRUTH IN ADVERTISING

And we all . . . are being transformed into his image with ever-increasing glory, which comes from the Lord, who is the Spirit.

2 CORINTHIANS 3:18

A sleek luxury car glides around hairpin turns. Skiers speed through sunlit powder. Majestic mountain peaks loom in the background on product packaging. Sleek, stylized images of mountains—just a couple of lines drawn at the proper angle—can represent a particular food brand or clothing line. Some products are even named for a particular peak. Advertisers understand the various ways the mountains appeal to us: adventure, stability, the purity of nature. Food, beverage, and clothing companies have all made use of mountains, as have banks and insurance agencies.

Do these products really have anything to do with the mountains they evoke? Maybe. Maybe not. Do the people who buy those products really hike or ski or climb—whatever the implied activity is? Probably some do, but many don't. There's nothing wrong with that in the realm of sales and branding. As long as the ads and logos are recognizable and appeal to consumers, they are considered a success. But God operates a bit differently.

God is exactly who He says He is. He reveals Himself to us through Scripture, in Jesus' life here on earth, and by the presence of the Holy Spirit in our day-to-day lives. In John 15, Jesus said, "I am the true vine, and my Father is the gardener. He cuts off every branch in me that bears no fruit, while every branch that does bear fruit he prunes so that it will be even more fruitful. . . . I am the vine; you are the branches. If you remain in me and I in you, you will bear much fruit; apart from me you can do nothing" (vv. 1–2, 5).

When we follow Jesus, it's not just a label or a logo. He transforms us from the inside out. As we walk with Him, we become more and more like Him, and our life shows it!

Thank You, Lord, for Your patience and persistence. Please continue shaping me to be more like You. I want You to shine through me!

EAGLES' FLIGHT

*"Does the eagle soar at your command and build its nest on high? It
dwells on a cliff and stays there at night; a rocky crag is its stronghold.
From there it looks for food; its eyes detect it from afar."*

JOB 39:27–29

Eagles are impressive birds. These verses capture it well, where it lives and how it hunts. Today we have live webcams in eagles' nests, and we can pull up a video online anytime we like. It's easy to forget that, not so long ago, a glimpse into an eagle's nest would have been a rare thing, accessible only after a daring climb.

We find other familiar verses about eagles in Isaiah: "He gives strength to the weary and increases the power of the weak. Even youths grow tired and weary, and young men stumble and fall; but those who hope in the LORD will renew their strength. They will soar on wings like eagles; they will run and not grow weary, they will walk and not be faint" (40:29–31).

Eagles soar seemingly without effort, gliding far and high with hardly a flap of their wings. That's because they are riding thermals, rising columns of warm air that carry them. Likewise, it's not our effort that renews our strength. The Lord gives us strength so that we can keep going long after we expected to drop in our tracks.

Two of David's psalms include similar themes. In Psalm 103, he describes many reasons to praise God. Verses 2–5 say, "Praise the LORD, my soul, and forget not all his benefits—who forgives all your sins and heals all your diseases, who redeems your life from the pit and crowns you with love and compassion, who satisfies your desires with good things so that your youth is renewed like the eagle's." That is quite a list of benefits! Psalm 27 concludes with sound advice: "Wait for the LORD; be strong and take heart and wait for the LORD" (v. 14).

Dear Father, thank You for the beautiful variety of birds You have created. Thank You for the inspiring flight of the eagle. Thank You that You care for us and renew our strength as we serve You.

MOUNTAINS
ON THE MOVE

Why, mountains, did you leap like rams, you hills, like lambs? Tremble,
earth, at the presence of the Lord, at the presence of the God of Jacob.

PSALM 114:6–7

Have you watched rams and lambs? Or seen videos online? Sheep can jump surprisingly well. Lambs leap, kick, buck, and twist across a field! Their legs almost seem to be spring-loaded as they jump, bounce, and run. It's surprising and comical to see the energy that surges through them.

This verse can bring to mind a silly cartoon, with legs and hooves sprouting beneath mountain peaks, then bouncing across the screen and off into the distance. But think of the mountains you know best, whether they are the red rock of the desert, rolling green hills, snow-capped peaks, or something else entirely! Whether you admire them from a distance or have hiked every trail, can you imagine them skipping like lambs? It no longer feels silly—surreal, perhaps, but also frightening.

Psalm 114 is talking about the power of our God, displayed in various ways when He brought Israel out of Egypt and into the Promised Land. Verses 6 and 7 refer to Exodus 19: "Mount Sinai was covered with smoke, because the LORD descended on it in fire. The smoke billowed up from it like smoke from a furnace, and the whole mountain trembled violently" (v. 18). God descended to Mount Sinai to speak to Moses in front of all the Israelites, to give them the Ten Commandments and other instructions. That's what made the mountains leap!

How mighty is our God! We are blessed to know Him, to worship One so strong and so loving.

O Lord, You are the Almighty One. You are powerful over all creation, even vast things like the mountains and the sea. I worship You, and I rest in Your loving care.

TRANSFIGURATION

Peter said to Jesus, "Lord, it is good for us to be here. If you wish, I will put up three shelters—one for you, one for Moses and one for Elijah."

MATTHEW 17:4

How often did Peter say and do exactly what we might have done—if we'd been there and had the nerve? He walked on water, after all! It seems like he was always running ahead or sticking his foot in his mouth. At times he probably felt foolish, as when he cut off the servant's ear in the Garden of Gethsemane.

In Matthew 17, Jesus took Peter, James, and John up on a high mountain by themselves. While they were there, "he was transfigured before them. His face shone like the sun, and his clothes became as white as the light" (v. 2).

Can you imagine what it would have been like to see that? Just being one of Jesus' disciples must have been extraordinary to begin with . . . but to see Him transformed in that way is impossible to grasp. Then, as if that weren't enough, Moses and Elijah appeared and started talking with Jesus!

Who can blame Peter for losing his head? He was so entranced, he wanted to put up shelters for Jesus, Moses, and Elijah so they could all stay there.

It's unlikely that any of us has experienced anything to match what Peter saw that day. But like Peter, we often want to linger too long in our own mountain-top experiences. Scripture does not record the details of what Jesus, Elijah, and Moses talked about, but you can be sure there was a purpose for their conversation. God has a purpose for each of our mountaintop experiences, too. It may be to strengthen our faith or teach us something new. Maybe He wants to expand our vision or clarify our understanding of who He is. There are countless possibilities.

Whatever gift God has for us, we can't stop time and bathe in it indefinitely. We have to absorb it and trek back down the mountain to our everyday reality, where our new understanding can influence our whole life. That's what it's for.

O Lord, thank You for the encouraging, hope-renewing mountaintop experiences You have given me. May those lessons bear fruit in my life always!

MOTORBOATS
AND CANOES

"Come to me, all you who are weary and burdened, and I will give you rest. Take my yoke upon you and learn from me, for I am gentle and humble in heart, and you will find rest for your souls. For my yoke is easy and my burden is light."

MATTHEW 11:28–30

Imagine for a moment that you're sitting in a deck chair at a riverside cabin. It's late in the afternoon, and the water is smooth and tranquil in this stretch of river. There's no noise of traffic or even airplanes overhead. The only sounds are birdsongs, the whisper of the breeze in the branches of nearby trees, and an occasional fish jumping. From time to time you see wildlife at the water's edge: herons, deer, red-winged blackbirds.

Occasionally a boat passes by on the water. You can hear the motorboats coming for a few minutes before they appear, their engines slowly growing louder until they finally come around the bend, sometimes coming upstream, sometimes going downstream. The people wave if they notice you there. The person at the tiller is watching ahead, steering carefully. They quickly pass out of sight. As the sound of the motor fades, the wake from their boat sloshes at the dock.

Other boats, canoes and kayaks and drift boats, are so quiet that you'll know they're coming only if the people are talking or laughing. They are almost always drifting downstream, gliding with the current. The people may be fishing. And they are apt to be silent, looking around, drinking in all that they see. If you happen to be reading when they pass by, you might not notice them at all.

Both types of boats have their uses. If someone were lost or injured and needed help, you'd want the motorboat for sure. A lot of our time is spent zipping along like that motorboat. But when we need renewal, the canoe quietly gliding downstream is just the ticket.

We can seek similar renewal in prayer and meditation. The current of the Living Water carries us as we rest. We listen. He reminds us of His love for us. He soothes our fractious minds and binds up our wounded and weary hearts. He gives us rest.

Thank You, Lord, for the rest that You give me. Your kindness and gentleness heal me. I yield to you.

SCARS AND SIGNPOSTS

My flesh and my heart may fail, but God is the
strength of my heart and my portion forever.

PSALM 73:26

Back in the day, trails, forest roads, and boundary lines were often marked by blazed trees, at least at first. Formal signs took time, but it took just a few strokes of an ax by a skilled axman to blaze a tree. First, he would make a horizontal cut through the bark at about shoulder height, into the outer layer of wood, called the cambium layer. Then higher on the trunk, he would make a downward cut slightly angled into the tree. Where the second cut met the first one, an outward thrust of the axe blade popped off the bark and a thin piece of the cambium. Sap oozed out and formed a protective covering. The blaze would heal as the tree grew, but the scar could be seen for many years, clearly marking the trail or the boundary line.

We have scars too, don't we? Some are on the outside, reminding us of an injury or a surgeon's work. Other scars are internal, in our minds, hearts, or spirits. Scars remind us that God offers us the strength to recover. "We do not have a high priest who is unable to empathize with our weaknesses, but we have one who has been tempted in every way, just as we are—yet he did not sin. Let us then approach God's throne of grace with confidence, so that we may receive mercy and find grace to help us in our time of need" (Hebrews 4:15–16).

God also equips us to help others heal as we have healed. "Praise be to the God and Father of our Lord Jesus Christ, the Father of compassion and the God of all comfort, who comforts us in all our troubles, so that we can comfort those in any trouble with the comfort we ourselves receive from God" (2 Corinthians 1:3–4). Whether we're on a trail in the woods or navigating life's challenges, it's heartening to know that others have gone before us and can show us the way.

Father, thank You for Your kindness to me. Thank You for those who have helped me find my way in life. Please help me to recognize when I can help someone else in turn.

BEING KNOWN

One of those days Jesus went out to a mountainside to pray, and spent
the night praying to God. When morning came, he called his disciples to
him and chose twelve of them, whom he also designated apostles.

LUKE 6:12–13

C hoosing His twelve disciples from among all His followers must have been one of the biggest decisions Jesus had to make during His ministry. The parallel passage in Mark says that "he appointed twelve that they might be with him and that he might send them out to preach and to have authority to drive out demons" (Mark 3:14–15). These men were to have a lot of responsibility, and they would be the beginning of the church.

When we hire employees, there are all kinds of strategies and metrics for choosing the best candidates. Whole industries have been built around growing your career and achieving your dreams. In spite of all that money and effort, getting hired still often comes down to who you know that has influence.

In a sense, that's exactly how the twelve got their positions. Not who they knew, but rather who knew them. God knew their hearts, and Jesus turned to the Father as He prepared to choose His closest followers. He spent the night praying, probably seeking His Father's counsel, and then He named His inner circle.

To our limited, human eyes, none of them really looked like ideal candidates. They were a motley bunch professionally and politically. Some went on to write gospel accounts and letters that we still read today in the New Testament. Some were prominent leaders in the early church, according to the book of Acts. Others faded from view. Does that mean that they were failures? Not at all. It just means that we don't know their whole story. But just as God knew their hearts, He also knows how they served throughout their lives.

God knows our hearts, too. He understands how we can serve Him, and He knows every bit of service and obedience that we are already giving. Other people may not know, and that's okay. The One we serve sees all our efforts.

Dear Father, thank You that You know me. Please guide me in how You want me to serve and obey You. Your opinion is the one that matters most to me by far.

EVER CHANGING,
EVER NEW

He set the earth on its foundations; it can never be moved. . . . How many are
your works, Lord! In wisdom you made them all; the earth is full of your creatures.

PSALM 104:5, 24

This is a beautiful planet that God created, isn't it? One of the joys of going outdoors is seeing new things. A hike or a mountain bike ride can bring us the delight of discovering someplace unfamiliar. From a high peak, there's a whole different view. We can see farther across the landscape. It spreads out before us: distant ridges and valleys, lakes and roads that we can't see from below. The sheer *distance* is breathtaking. Familiar landmarks are often made strange, seen from so far away, so high above.

Or maybe the place you've come to is itself the discovery: a sunlit lake. A majestic waterfall pouring over a cliff. A meadow spangled with wildflowers. Wildlife can be a delightful discovery too. Silent, graceful deer nibbling at the brush. An unfamiliar birdsong. An otter swimming in a river. An osprey swooping to catch a fish. Even the vegetation can offer surprises, like a wildflower you've never seen before. What a delight to find so much that is new and beautiful in the natural world!

Thanks to the seasons and weather patterns, even the same spot can appear new again and again. Vibrant green clothes the hills in springtime. Autumn sets the foliage aflame. The same mountain, the same valley, the same river, or the same tree we've seen a hundred times before shows us a new face and a new mood as the light changes or the snow falls. God is so good to us to create such beauty to share. His creativity never ends.

Father God, Your creativity is unending! Thank You for making our world an ever-changing delight.

DAILY BREAD

"Give us today our daily bread."

MATTHEW 6:11

Can you imagine living near the mountains and never going to them? Never hiking or biking the trails. Never going camping or even having a picnic in a meadow. Never swimming in a lake or hiking to a waterfall. Never skiing or snowboarding or sledding or tubing. It sounds crazy, doesn't it?

Yet for many of us, it seems that the only time we go to the "must see" attractions in our area is when we have visitors from out of town! We may live near the beach, or perhaps our town boasts a renowned theater, a famous museum, or a major sports arena. We know that we can go anytime . . . and yet we never do.

It's easy to take good things for granted when we know they're always available, isn't it? If we're not careful, this attitude can even infect our relationship with God. Maybe that's why, when the disciples asked Jesus to teach them to pray, His instructions included basic things. Obvious things.

"Give us today our daily bread."

It doesn't get much more everyday than that, does it? This basic, daily, physical need is right in the middle between parts of the prayer that we might think of as more spiritual. The beginning of the prayer praises God and yields to Him. The end of the prayer asks for forgiveness and protection from evil. In the middle is this request for daily sustenance.

Here's one little lesson we can take from the Lord's Prayer. Worshipping God and receiving forgiveness are just as vital to our daily lives as food is. They might be easier to overlook, but spiritually, we starve without them.

Let's take time today to thank God for the blessings we take for granted!

O Lord, You are holy God. Please provide for my spiritual needs as well as my physical needs. Please forgive me where I have missed the mark. Thank You.

FOCUS

*For everything that was written in the past was written to teach
us, so that through the endurance taught in the Scriptures and
the encouragement they provide we might have hope.*

ROMANS 15:4

When we first set out on a trail, we're often thinking about the goal ahead, the distance we have to go, or what we might see along the way. It's exciting to leave the trailhead behind and begin to climb. We're grateful for the people who built and maintain the trail. We may even wonder who else has hiked this path. But sometimes as we continue on, our focus narrows to the few steps in front of us. Maybe our feet start to hurt. All we see is the next small portion of the trail.

Life can be like that. We get focused on the task at hand and forget about the larger picture. Instead of turning to God, we think our time is better spent working on the problem ourselves. We fall into thinking that the issue we are dealing with will go on forever, and we grow discouraged.

God cares about the details of our daily lives. Psalm 46:1 tells us, "God is our refuge and strength, an ever-present help in trouble."

Whatever the problem is, His Word can help us get through it. Perhaps there's a passage that speaks directly to our struggle. Maybe reading about how a biblical figure dealt with something similar will show us how to respond to our situation. (Or how not to!) Even if our specific circumstance is not addressed in Scripture, the Psalms can comfort us by giving voice to our fears and frustrations. We can pray those verses to the Lord too.

*Dear Father God, help me to remember to turn to You with my
problems. Thank You for caring about my struggles. Thank
You for giving us Your Word. You are a loving Father!*

HUNGRY

Like newborn babies, crave pure spiritual milk, so that by it you may grow up in your salvation, now that you have tasted that the Lord is good.

1 PETER 2:2–3

There's just something about camping that sharpens the appetite. Maybe it's being outdoors. Maybe it's the physical activity of hiking and setting up camp. Maybe it's the fact that meals tend to be planned; there's not a full freezer or pantry to graze from. Maybe it's being just a little bit cold.

We eat differently on a camping trip too. That doesn't necessarily mean we're eating any healthier! There's usually no fridge, which means it's difficult to keep produce fresh. Unless we've brought an RV, there's probably no microwave. We have to actually light a burner and wait for water to boil. We have to watch the food, pay attention, whether it's on a Coleman stove or inside a Dutch oven sitting on coals. There's no "Ding!" of a microwave to tell us our food is ready.

Feeding ourselves is one of the major tasks of human life. It's one of the reasons we work for a living. "By the sweat of your brow you will eat your food" (Genesis 3:19).

Feeding our mind and our soul is work as well. Oh, it's easy to graze on mental junk food, whatever that looks like for each of us. We live in a time and place of abundant information. We can easily find empty calories . . . or wise, nutrient-rich resources. Are we giving ourselves good spiritual nutrition?

Paul talks about some believers needing to drink spiritual milk, as they are not ready for meat. (See 1 Corinthians 3.) Wherever we are, we can reach for the most nourishing food we can stomach, and grow stronger in our faith.

Thank You, Father God, for my taste buds. Thank you for the way my appetite is sharpened by fresh air and physical activity. Thank You for providing so many tasty, nourishing things for me to consume—physically, mentally, emotionally, and spiritually!

MOUNTAIN GOATS

The high mountains are for the wild goats; the rocks are a refuge for the rock badgers.

PSALM 104:18 ESV

Mountain goats live high in the mountains of western North America, and they are uniquely designed for life on steep, rocky slopes. Their white, double-layered winter coats hold heat but repel wind and water, so they can tolerate high winds and temperatures down to minus fifty degrees Fahrenheit. They eat a wide variety of alpine vegetation, including lichen. Their split hooves spread wide apart for balance, and softer inner pads provide traction. They have very strong necks, shoulders, and front legs. As a result, they can go right up slopes as steep as sixty degrees! They can climb quickly and elude many predators, including wolves and bears. (Of course, cougars and golden eagles are not deterred much by the steep terrain.) Strangely enough, mountain goats would not survive as well in gentler places. On flat ground, they are too slow to escape from predators.

There is a lesson to be gleaned from the life of mountain goats. God gives us what we need too. We don't always recognize it. All too often we wish we had someone else's gifts. But God has distributed His gifts as He sees fit. To sulk or to pine for what He gave someone else shows ingratitude. We are all different, yet each one of us is loved by the Creator and created for His purpose and His pleasure.

The Lord has put us where we are for a reason. He wants to touch this world through us. We don't want to miss the adventure He planned just for us!

O Lord, thank You for how You have made me and where You have put me. Please help me to put two and two together, and see how I can serve You here!

RETURNING
TO THE SPRING

*He said to me: "It is done. I am the Alpha and the Omega, the Beginning and the
End. To the thirsty I will give water without cost from the spring of the water of life."*

REVELATION 21:6

How delightful it is to drink from a mountain spring. The water is often pure,
clear, and cool. No wonder a good spring can be a primary selling point in a
real estate transaction! From the book of Genesis, where the river flowed out from
the Garden of Eden (2:10) to the book of Revelation (21:6), God uses springs as a
way to show that He gives and sustains life.

It is not surprising that the children of Israel grumbled when they were trav-
eling through the wilderness and thirst overcame them. How relieved they must
have been when the Lord told Moses to strike the rock and water came out! (See
Exodus 17:1–7.) God was showing them His power over creation and His care
for them.

In Psalm 1 and in Jeremiah 17, the person who trusts in the Lord or delights
in His law is compared to a tree by a stream. "They will be like a tree planted by
the water that sends out its roots by the stream. It does not fear when heat comes;
its leaves are always green. It has no worries in a year of drought and never fails to
bear fruit" (Jeremiah 17:8).

When we seek the Lord, especially by opening and reading His Word, He provides us with living water. Jesus Himself offered it to the woman at the well, and
she didn't understand at first (John 4). We may smile at her confusion, but we've all
had times when we found ourselves far from the Lord and needed to return to the
water of life. Thankfully, the Lord welcomes us back again and again.

*Lord, thank You for providing living water. May I
drink deeply from it and know Your great love for me!*

MANY ROUTES

Show me your ways, Lord, teach me your paths. Guide me in your truth
and teach me, for you are God my Savior, and my hope is in you all day long.

PSALM 25:4–5

There are many ways for roads to get past a mountain range. Some highways go up and over a pass, winding back and forth to gain elevation until cresting the top, and then winding back down the other side. In a few places, a tunnel has been bored straight through the mountain, taking drivers on a shorter—though darker— route. Sometimes, the road doesn't even cross the mountains at all; it may swing far out of the way to avoid them altogether.

Who knows how those routes were planned? There were probably many factors: time, money, accessible technology, the land available, and the preferences of an engineer or government official.

When obstacles and trials loom on our horizons, God may bring us through them in many different ways. His creativity isn't limited to our lovely physical world. He also holds infinite possibilities in how our journeys unfold and how He leads us through them. Of course, we always hope He'll take us by way of the road that curves far out of the way to avoid the trials. Who wants to go looking for trouble?

If we think of a trial as a mountain, the tunnel sounds like a quick and safe route—unless you're claustrophobic. In that case, you may breathe easier on the road over the pass, even though it takes longer. On the other hand, travelers who are afraid of heights would probably prefer the shelter of the tunnel. Someone who's impatient might loathe taking the long way around, but one who's dreading arriving at the destination would welcome it.

Not that we always get what we wish for, right? God may allow His claustrophobic child to avoid the tunnel or He might take the child right into it and guide her safely through. God knows our fears, our wounds, our weaknesses. No matter what route He leads us on, He is God of the mountain.

Dear Lord, I am grateful that we don't all have to follow identical paths. Lead me where You want me to go. I trust You!

UPROOTED

After Job had prayed for his friends, the LORD restored his
fortunes and gave him twice as much as he had before.

JOB 42:10

The tall, strong tree growing along the riverbank looks sturdy. We imagine the roots spreading out, giving a firm foundation. It looks like the tree will remain standing for many years to come. Then, a fast snowmelt or a heavy rain leads to a flood. The bank is undercut, and the tree falls into the water and washes downstream. It may get wedged against the bank and form a bridge or logjam, or just a small diversion of the stream. Fish and other aquatic creatures enjoy the shade and the quiet pool that is formed.

If the tree is carried all the way to the mouth of the river where it empties into a lake or the ocean, it may float for a long time before washing up on the shore and becoming driftwood. Many artists prize this washed wood. The bark and most of the limbs have usually been beaten off during the journey, and the log may have been naturally sanded into strange shapes. The wood can be used in a fire pit on the beach, where friends and family can enjoy cooking, warmth, and fellowship. Other driftwood protects a portion of the beach, gives shore birds a place to perch, or simply adds beauty to the scene.

We too can find that our life, which seems stable and strong, may be suddenly uprooted. We may have to leave our familiar, comfortable surroundings and be thrust into uncertainty. Perhaps we end up far away from where we thought we were putting down roots. Life has changed.

While we sometimes have no control over events in our life, we can usually choose how to respond to them. We have the option of looking for ways to grow and improve. Although the trials and the turmoil are real and may be sorrowful, the restoration can be joyful. Eventually, like Job, we may find ourselves doing even better than before. When we look back later, we may be amazed and grateful to see how God used the upheaval on our journey for His glory and for our good.

Lord, sometimes life overwhelms me. Thank You that You are always there. May I always be compliant toward You and looking for Your blessing.

WIND

"You should not be surprised at my saying, 'You must be born again.' The wind blows wherever it pleases. You hear its sound, but you cannot tell where it comes from or where it is going. So it is with everyone born of the Spirit."

JOHN 3:7–8

The White Mountains of New Hampshire and Maine feature some rugged territory. For more than sixty years, New Hampshire's Mount Washington held the record for the fastest wind gust ever recorded on Earth. The 231-mile-per-hour gust was recorded on April 12, 1934, at the Mount Washington Observatory, and it still stands as the strongest recorded in the Western Hemisphere and the Northern Hemisphere. The observatory sits at an elevation of 6,288 feet, and for a variety of reasons, it experiences some amazingly bad weather.

Across our planet, the wind does many things. It plays a part in complex weather patterns; it provides wind power; it gives life to sailboats; and gentler winds help pollinate plants, to name just a few of its functions.

So it is with the Holy Spirit. We do not see Him, yet His effects are felt in countless ways. Think of how many believers there are all over the world. Now consider that the Holy Spirit is within each one, helping us, comforting us, counseling us, and reminding us of all that Jesus taught. He empowers us. He envelops us in love and cultivates in us His fruit: "love, joy, peace, forbearance, kindness, goodness, faithfulness, gentleness and self-control" (Galatians 5:22–23). We cannot see the Spirit, yet the evidence of His presence is everywhere.

Praise God for His generosity in being present with us in this powerful way!

O Lord, thank You for transforming my life through the Holy Spirit. Your ways are so wise and so loving! Help me to recognize Your presence and to freely cooperate with You.

REFUGE

In the LORD I take refuge. How then can you say to
me: "Flee like a bird to your mountain"?

PSALM 11:1

Sometimes it seems like the world has gone topsy-turvy, that our foundation is sliding out from under us whether it's in our family, our church, our nation, our culture, or our professional lives. In those seasons, our desire to head out to the mountains may feel less like a joyful renewal and more like a desperate escape! As Psalm 11:3 says, "When the foundations are being destroyed, what can the righteous do?"

David gave a steady response to that panicked question: "In the LORD I take refuge. . . . The LORD is in his holy temple; the LORD is on his heavenly throne" (vv. 1, 4). In fact, he asked a question in return: *How can you say this to me?* He was not flustered by the circumstances around him that just seemed so wrong.

It may be that those who told David to flee had forgotten the true source of their safety. Their security was resting on human order. When that order was threatened, they forgot that God was still on His throne. He is still the safest refuge. He is the ultimate source of justice.

Another psalmist wrote, "Those who trust in the LORD are like Mount Zion, which cannot be shaken but endures forever. As the mountains surround Jerusalem, so the LORD surrounds his people both now and forevermore" (Psalm 125:1–2).

When things feel shaky, the best thing to do is to turn to the One who is the same yesterday, today, and forever.

Father God, thank You for offering me refuge. Sometimes I am
distressed by what goes on in this world. Please hold me close
and steady when everything seems to be crumbling around me

BUILDING

And it will be said: "Build up, build up, prepare the road!
Remove the obstacles out of the way of my people."

ISAIAH 57:14

When the first transcontinental railroad was built, the progress through the Sierra Nevada was excruciatingly slow. The day's work was often measured in inches as several tunnels were dug through the mountains. During the harsh winter of 1866–1867, workers had to clear several feet of snow to bring supplies to the thousands of men who were drilling and blasting, laying ties and track. There was danger from explosions, cave-ins, and avalanches.

It took four years to breach the Sierra Nevada. Six years after the project was started, the rail lines from the east and west met at Promontory Summit, Utah Territory. One of the inscriptions on the golden spike used in the ceremony read, "May God continue the unity of our country as this railroad unites the two great oceans of the world."

Building anything takes time, and the bigger and more complex the project is, the more effort and time it will require. In Ephesians, Paul gave us an idea of just how ambitious God is for His church: "So Christ himself gave the apostles, the prophets, the evangelists, the pastors and teachers, to equip his people for works of service, so that the body of Christ may be built up until we all reach unity in the faith and in the knowledge of the Son of God and become mature, attaining to the whole measure of the fullness of Christ" (Ephesians 4:11–13). That sounds like an almost impossible ideal, doesn't it?

As with any long-term endeavor, we just have to keep taking the next step. In 1 Thessalonians 5:11, we are shown one key task: to "encourage one another and build each other up, just as in fact you are doing." This building up can take many forms:

a kind word spoken at the right time; a hot meal cooked during a family's illness or grief; or a letter to a member of the military serving far from home. The cost may be great or small, but the encouragement can have consequences beyond our lifetime.

Lord, I want to become more like You. Please equip me for that; I can't do it on my own. Please help me to encourage my brothers and sisters and build them up.

TIME WITH GOD

Now when Jesus saw the crowds, he went up on a mountainside and
sat down. His disciples came to him, and he began to teach them.

MATTHEW 5:1–2

Jesus often went up on a mountain to pray or to teach. We may feel like we are climbing a mountain every day as we try to get on top of all the things that eat up our time. We have to rush here and there—to work, to school, to meetings, to run errands. We are so busy that we often miss out on the opportunity to spend time with the Lord. But on the days when we put aside all other demands and spend time with God, we are blessed. Whether we turn to Him for a few minutes in the morning, spend an hour reading the Scriptures and praying, or do an in-depth Bible study lesson, we often receive an unexpected peace. This gift from God is described in Philippians 4:7: "And the peace of God, which transcends all understanding, will guard your hearts and your minds in Christ Jesus."

Our progress toward any goal is usually in direct proportion to the time and effort we put into it. It's no different as we develop the habit of spending time with God. We reap what we sow. Each goal we set and reach may not seem like much in itself, but when we look back, it's like looking down from the top of a mountain we have just climbed. In fact, it takes a desire and a commitment similar to that of physically climbing a mountain peak. We know it will be worth the effort, but when we reach the goal, we are astonished by just how sweet it is.

Dear Lord, I am often overwhelmed by the daily
pressures of life. Please help me find the time to be
still and listen to You. I treasure my time with You.

THE SOURCE

Come, let us sing for joy to the LORD; let us shout aloud to the Rock of our salvation. Let us come before him with thanksgiving and extol him with music and song. For the LORD is the great God, the great King above all gods. In his hand are the depths of the earth, and the mountain peaks belong to him.

PSALM 95:1–4

T he outdoors are a gift from God, part of His abundance. They are alive because He is the source of all life. God breathed life into Adam, and the trees, vines, bushes, and grass that produce oxygen are from Him. The Lord is our Rock, and the soil that anchors and nurtures plant life, that houses animals in dens, came from Him. He is the Light of the world, and the sunshine that warms all life, that thaws ice and makes it possible for plants to generate oxygen, was created by Him. He is the true Vine, and the birds and bats, bees and other insects that pollinate plants are His creations. He gives us the water of life, and the streams and rivers that teem with fish and other water dwellers are from Him. The mountains that hold snow, saving up water for the land and crops, were designed by Him. The rain that waters the earth is a gift from Him.

The Lord has given us life in so many ways. He created us. He sustains us, "for in him we live and move and have our being" (Acts 17:28). He brought us eternal life in salvation. He is the source of all our life, on every level, and He is worthy of our praise.

O Lord my Creator, I am awed by all that You have made. Thank You for the abundant life You give. Thank You for the astonishing variety of life on our planet! Help us to be wise and compassionate in how we behave toward Your world.

GENTLE PATHS

He tends his flock like a shepherd: He gathers the lambs in his arms and
carries them close to his heart; he gently leads those that have young.

Isaiah 40:11

We do need gentle leading, don't we? How wise our Good Shepherd is! He doesn't push us along steep slopes where we would stumble and fall. Rather, He leads us where the footing is softer, beside quiet waters and along the right paths.

Sometimes we get frustrated and impatient with God. We think we know where He wants to take us. Our destination is there in the distance, drawing our gaze like a high mountain peak, and it doesn't seem to be getting any closer. Oh, we are walking and walking and walking, but it seems like the Lord is leading us back and forth, back and forth over the same ground again and again, rather than taking us directly to the goal. If you think God is slow to fulfill His purposes for you, remember how long Abraham and Sarah waited for Isaac!

We may be missing the fact that those paths we're tramping back and forth are switchbacks—that with every turn in the road, we are gaining elevation, getting closer to our goal. It may be that we don't understand just how steep the "direct route" would be or how risky.

Our impatience does nothing for us. God's timing is simply not the same as ours. We must trust that He has a purpose to His pacing. David wisely wrote, "Teach me to do your will, for you are my God; may your good Spirit lead me on level ground" (Psalm 143:10).

The Lord is our Shepherd, and we can trust Him to lead us.

O Lord, my Shepherd, I will follow You. Please forgive me for my impatience or thinking I know better than You do. You are the Good Shepherd; I yield to Your guidance!

FISHING

"Come, follow me," Jesus said, "and I will send you out to fish for people."

MARK 1:17

The high mountain lakes are often good places to fish, especially if we have to hike a ways to get there. A person will frequently find himself all alone at a hidden lake. Even when we don't catch anything, there is a peacefulness that comes while waiting for a bite.

Whether we use a willow stick or an expensive fly rod, there is the chance that a fish might take the bait. Sometimes it doesn't take much to improve our luck. Moving to a different location can do it, and so can switching to another bait. Even a slight change in the weather can bring the fish out.

When we share our faith with others or pray for the salvation of a loved one, patience is required. The Holy Spirit is the One who draws a person to the Savior. It is not our cleverness or fancy bait that draws people in. We don't need years of schooling or a flawless presentation to tell what God has done for us. As a witness, we tell what we have experienced, what the facts are, and how our life has changed. Some of us may not have a dramatic backstory, but all believers can share the goodness of God and how we have grown to depend on Him. Others may be struggling with the same problems we've had; some of them will listen.

When our openness about the Lord helps another person turn to Him, we end up being blessed. We discover that we were made fishers of men.

Lord, please help me to speak freely of all that You have done for me. I would like others to know You as well, to experience the forgiveness, cleansing, and healing that You offer. Please guide me to speak honestly and kindly.

TRAIL CLEARING

He has shown you, O mortal, what is good. And what does the LORD require
of you? To act justly and to love mercy and to walk humbly with your God.

MICAH 6:8

Every trail must be maintained if it is going to be used. Trees and limbs can fall across the path during storms. Water erodes the walkway. Rocks work their way to the surface. All of these things get in the way and make the trail less safe. They could even cause injury if we are not careful.

How true this is in our lives. Events both large and small can interrupt our daily walk. The way we want to go may be blocked by a lack of resources or ability. A wrong choice may have diverted us from the straight and narrow path we started on when we came to know the Lord.

For this reason, the Lord reminded us to stop, rest, and turn our eyes upon Him. We can do this in many ways. It can be as quick as a few minutes of rest and meditation during a coffee break or as routine as the sleep we get each night. Gathering with other believers on Sunday—or any other day—may become a weekly time to slow down and refocus. Communion can be a time of particular refreshment. So can a vacation. These times of rest and spiritual cleansing do us a world of good.

We can clear our thoughts, our hearts, and our souls of anything that interferes with our worship. We might use this time to look back and reflect. Perhaps we need to change direction. When we use our time in prayer to confess, we are grateful for the many promises of God's forgiveness, such as 1 John 1:9. The Lord's willingness to keep cleansing us again and again demonstrates that He knows us and loves us. He wants us to continue walking with Him.

Thank You, God, for the way You made me. Please help me to notice times when I can pause, be still, and turn to You. May I walk humbly with You.

CHALLENGE

I praise you because I am fearfully and wonderfully made;
your works are wonderful, I know that full well.

PSALM 139:14

One of the joys of life is how amazing our bodies are. Even the most average of us learns to do extraordinary things: to stand and walk, to reach, to grasp objects, to throw a ball, to run, to jump, to roll and scramble and climb.

The natural world offers so many ways to take that joy and kick it up a notch. We feel the sun and wind on our skin. We walk on the soft dirt or grass. We climb trees or mountains for the joy of climbing and to see a new vista. We bicycle and ski and snowshoe.

Whether you're an athlete taking on a rigorous new challenge or someone with limited mobility, we can all stretch our abilities and savor the outdoors. Maybe there's a new skill you want to master—the challenge of rock climbing or a technical mountain bike trail. Perhaps you're ready to push yourself to the next level. Maybe you want to stay as active and strong as possible as you age. With adaptive sports organizations, the outdoors open up for those of us with disabilities. There are countless reasons and ways to nudge ourselves to do just a little bit more.

Some of us have additional goals when we venture out, such as the homeschooling parent on a field trip teaching her child outdoor sports for physical education as well as studying biology or geology in the field. Someone recovering from an injury may train in the fresh air for his physical therapy. Youth leaders teach survival skills and teamwork to young people.

No matter what our needs are and what we have to offer, God has provided a glorious world to enjoy.

Thank You, Lord, for my body and for this world You created.
Help me push myself to develop my physical abilities. If I am far
from nature, please give me the opportunity to get out and enjoy
it and to catch the glimpses available right here, where I live.

LOST

"Suppose one of you has a hundred sheep and loses one of them. Doesn't he leave the ninety-nine in the open country and go after the lost sheep until he finds it? And when he finds it, he joyfully puts it on his shoulders and goes home. Then he calls his friends and neighbors together and says, 'Rejoice with me; I have found my lost sheep.'"

LUKE 15:4–6

We've all lost things, sometimes small but important items like a list, an idea, or our car keys. It's so frustrating! Then there are irreplaceable items, like a cherished heirloom, that are of course more painful to lose. Maybe it was accidentally broken or lost in a move or a fire. Most frightening of all is when a family member goes missing, even for a few hours. We can grow frantic if his absence stretches on. How grateful we are when we are reunited with him! We can relate to that shepherd finding his lost sheep.

Another type of loss is the loss of fellowship, of peace, and of belonging. This is painful enough when it happens between people, but it is so much worse when those qualities are lost between us and God. When we think about this, we begin to understand the greatness of Jesus' sacrifice. As soon as we realize our need for a Savior, when we first believe, our lostness is over and we belong to Him.

In Ezekiel 34 we read, "I myself will tend my sheep and have them lie down, declares the Sovereign LORD. I will search for the lost and bring back the strays. I will bind up the injured and strengthen the weak" (vv. 15–16).

How delightful it is when salvation comes to someone we have been praying for! We can only imagine how they celebrate over that person in heaven.

O Lord, thank You for Your gift of salvation. Thank You for finding me when I was lost. Please continue to find those who are lost

FISHING AND FIREWOOD

As we have opportunity, let us do good to all people,
especially to those who belong to the family of believers.

GALATIANS 6:10

A retired couple owned a riverfront cabin in the woods. They often invited friends and family to gather there. When it was just the close family, the man spent his days either cutting firewood or fishing from his boat. Sometimes he and his buddies would take their pickups into the woods and get firewood together. They helped stock one another's woodpiles and also took firewood to widows and other needy families. Sometimes the man fished alone. Other times friends fished with him, or he took his grandchildren or other young relatives out in the boat.

One day the couple's little granddaughter asked her grandfather which he liked better, fishing or cutting firewood. No adult would ever ask that, would she? We'd assume the fishing was fun and relaxing, and cutting firewood was a tiresome chore. But that's not how the grandfather answered.

"Oh," he said, "I like fishing. It's nice to be out on the river. But I can only be out there for just so long. And then after a while, I find myself thinking, *You know, I'd just as soon be cutting wood.* So I come back in, get my gear, and go chop wood. And then I do that for just so long, and after a while, I find myself thinking, *You know, I'd just as soon be fishing!*"

We may chuckle at that, but this older man was using his time wisely. The fish helped feed his family and were given generously to others as well. The wood he cut heated the cabin, heated their home in town, and helped heat the homes of friends as well as widows, single moms, and other needy folks from church.

Whatever stage of life we're in, there is a place for us to help others. Even when we don't see an opening for our particular gifts, we can always pray for people.

O Lord, sometimes I don't see how I can offer anything to my brothers and sisters. Help me to recognize my opportunities to serve. Thank You for Your goodness to me!

UNLIKELY TREES

"I will put in the desert the cedar and the acacia, the myrtle and the olive.
I will set junipers in the wasteland, the fir and the cypress together, so that
people may see and know, may consider and understand, that the hand of
the LORD has done this, that the Holy One of Israel has created it."

ISAIAH 41:19–20

Trees growing in a forest may be mostly the same species, or they might be a mixture of several varieties. Some trees require specific conditions, and others seem to sprout up just about anywhere. Occasionally we are surprised to see a tree growing where it seems that nothing more than moss or lichen could survive. These trees, which seem to grow out of solid rock, do not grow quickly in trunk size. They don't reach high toward the heavens, and they don't produce a heavy cone crop. But they do serve a purpose.

The seed of that tree probably landed in a crack where just enough soil had collected to allow it to germinate. As the roots reached down, they most likely followed tiny cracks until they reached a source of water. The root system filled the cracks in the stone and started to spread them farther apart as the roots grew. The steady pressure forced the cracks open, allowing more soil and moisture to trickle down. The tree is helping break down the rock and form more soil.

We all know of missionaries and pastors who might feel like a tree growing in a rock. They may be trying to plant a church or grow a congregation in a hard, spiritually dry location. There may be a lot of resistance. They too are doing important work, sowing seeds that may take long years to show any noticeable growth. Proverbs 11:30 tells us, "The fruit of the righteous is a tree of life, and he who is wise wins souls" (NASB).

These pastors and missionaries need our encouragement. They may be thirsting for a kind word or a small gift from home. Sometimes a note will bless them more than we can imagine. And of course, we can pray for God's grace and provision for them.

O Lord, You show us amazing things in nature.
Please help me to pass on Your amazing love to others.

NO COMPETITION

God did not appoint us to suffer wrath but to receive salvation through our Lord Jesus Christ. He died for us so that, whether we are awake or asleep, we may live together with him. Therefore encourage one another and build each other up, just as in fact you are doing.

1 THESSALONIANS 5:9–11

When a group of people hike together or climb a peak, they don't need to race. The last person to finish the trail or reach the summit has arrived every bit as much as the first person. They are all able to have fun together, enjoy the view, and rest in their accomplishment.

That's kind of the way it is in our Christian life as well. There are many reasons for going to church, Bible study, or a small-group gathering; one important reason is to spend time with other believers. Even in the beginning, the Lord said, "It is not good for the man to be alone" (Genesis 2:18). While we may enjoy solitude, we have been made social creatures.

Hebrews 10:24–25 reminds us, "Let us consider how we may spur one another on toward love and good deeds, not giving up meeting together, as some are in the habit of doing, but encouraging one another." We are not in competition; we are working together.

But wait . . . 1 Corinthians 9:24–25 says, "Do you not know that in a race all the runners run, but only one gets the prize? Run in such a way as to get the prize. Everyone who competes in the games goes into strict training. They do it to get a crown that will not last, but we do it to get a crown that will last forever."

Does that mean we *are* in competition with one another? That only one gets the prize? While these verses at first seem to suggest that, Paul is really telling us that everyone can gain the prize of salvation and eternal life. We are each to do our best in whatever way we serve the Lord. The goal is to excel, not compete. All of us can look forward to that first glimpse of heaven.

Thank You, Lord, that following You is not a solo endeavor. Please help me to be an encouragement to my brothers and sisters!

DIFFERENT VEHICLES, DIFFERENT GIFTS

We have different gifts, according to the grace given to each of us. If your gift is prophesying, then prophesy in accordance with your faith; if it is serving, then serve; if it is teaching, then teach; if it is to encourage, then give encouragement; if it is giving, then give generously; if it is to lead, do it diligently; if it is to show mercy, do it cheerfully.

ROMANS 12:6–8

Mountain roads tend to wind their way along. Only occasionally will they have a long straight stretch. The terrain, broken by steep slopes and curving valleys and ravines, just doesn't lend itself to straight lines. The dramatic scenery and winding roads make for fun driving when the conditions are good. However, in bad weather, it's a different story.

Some high mountain roads get so much snow that they are closed during the winter. It costs too much to remove the deep snow, and ice on the curves makes driving too hazardous anyway. In the spring, it takes a long time to clear these roads. Sometimes just a single lane width of snow is removed, usually by very large snow blowers mounted on heavy equipment. While the remaining snow is melting, cyclists have the road to themselves. Even after all the snow is gone and the highway opens for the season, longer vehicles may be prohibited because of the steep and winding nature of the route. Not every vehicle is suited for every road.

In a similar manner, not every believer can do every type of ministry. But just as every type of vehicle has a purpose, so each of us has been given a gift. Our challenge is to discover our gift and find ways to use it.

Dear Father, thank You for all that You have given me. Please guide me in how I serve You.

MOUNTAIN TRAILS

Many peoples will come and say, "Come, let us go up to the
mountain of the LORD, to the temple of the God of Jacob. He
will teach us his ways, so that we may walk in his paths."

ISAIAH 2:3

Have you ever thought about the way a mountain can reflect our lifetime experiences? Our journey usually begins with education, which could be compared to the climb up a mountain. We base our current studies on what we learned before, just as our current location on the trail was achieved by starting at the base and walking up and up. We have a goal in education, a degree or a body of knowledge, just as we want to reach the top of the mountain. The same may be true in a career where we start out in an entry-level position and build on it.

Trails in the mountains often climb to a ridge and then descend a bit before ascending again. Similarly, life is made up of high points and sometimes coming back down to the valley. There may be times of great difficulty, even failure, and other days when we can rest by a quiet stream in the shade of a tree.

We can take heart from the fact that the Lord is with us on this journey. Hebrews 13:5–6 reminds us, "God has said, 'Never will I leave you; never will I forsake you.' So we say with confidence, 'The Lord is my helper; I will not be afraid.'"

Psalm 3:4 says, "I call out to the LORD, and he answers me from his holy mountain." We can respond with Psalm 99:9: "Exalt the LORD our God, and worship at his holy mountain; for the LORD our God is holy!" (ESV).

O Lord, sometimes life does feel like a mountain, much too
big for me to summit! Thank You that You provide rest along
the way and invite me to drink from Your pure streams.

WISDOM AND WATER

The words of a man's mouth are like deep waters [copious and
difficult to fathom]; the fountain of [mature, godly] wisdom is like
a bubbling stream [sparkling, fresh, pure, and life-giving].

PROVERBS 18:4 AMP

Proverbs 18:4 describes two different water sources as a way of contrasting two influences in our lives. People's words are described as "deep waters." Deep waters are unpredictable and potentially dangerous because you can't see what is hidden in those dark and murky depths. There may be something nourishing, such as fish, or there may be hidden hazards, perhaps a submerged rock, a venomous creature, or debris. The water may be stagnant and polluted, or there could be hidden currents.

In contrast to those deep waters, the fountain of wisdom is "like a bubbling stream." Brooks are fresh, ever-changing, providing habitat for fish and other creatures, as well as water to drink.

Where are we getting our spiritual water? Are we gulping down the words of others? If so, what makes them worth listening to? Do we pay attention just because they are famous, clever, or attractive? Are they wise, or are they just interesting talkers?

James wrote, "Who is wise and understanding among you? Let them show it by their good life, by deeds done in the humility that comes from wisdom. . . . The wisdom that comes from heaven is first of all pure; then peace-loving, considerate, submissive, full of mercy and good fruit, impartial and sincere" (James 3:13, 17). That gives us a pretty clear picture of what wisdom looks like. Do the people we listen to show those qualities?

It may take a bit of effort to seek out the bubbling stream of wisdom. However, James also wrote, "If any of you lacks wisdom, you should ask God, who gives generously to all without finding fault, and it will be given to you" (James 1:5). That's an encouraging promise!

Father, thank You that Your wisdom is pure and peace-loving. Please give me that wisdom today! Help me to realize what sort of "water" I am drinking.

MOUNTAINS OF MANY COLORS

Each of you should use whatever gift you have received to serve others, as faithful stewards of God's grace in its various forms. If anyone speaks, they should do so as one who speaks the very words of God. If anyone serves, they should do so with the strength God provides, so that in all things God may be praised through Jesus Christ.

1 PETER 4:10–11

The beloved song "America the Beautiful" mentions "purple mountain majesties" among God's blessings. Actually, many mountains around the world are named for the color they appear to be. There are the Green Mountains in Vermont and the White Mountains in New Hampshire. The Black Hills in South Dakota and Wyoming were so named by the Lakota because the thick ponderosa pine forests made them look black from a distance. Arizona has three different peaks called Red Mountain, not to be confused with the Red Mountain ski area in British Columbia. New South Wales, Australia, has the Blue Mountains, named for the haze that hangs above them. Similarly, the Cherokee called the Great Smoky Mountains "Shaconage," meaning "place of the blue smoke." In northwestern China, the Zhangye Danxia National Geological Park contains the Rainbow Mountains, with red peaks striped with various colors depending on the mineral content of the rock. People who have visited the Rainbow Mountains say that the colors are most vivid after a rainstorm. The variety of God's creation is stunning!

The Lord delights in His creation, whether it is the natural world or the people who inhabit it. The differences among us are also designed by God and are a reflection of Him. He gives each person different gifts, abilities, and opportunities to serve Him. Our purpose is to bring Him glory. Ephesians 5:26 reminds us that the church is made holy as it is cleansed "by the washing with water through the word." Just like those mountains, our ministry is more vibrant after a good cleansing!

Dear Lord, thank You that each of us has different gifts. Thank You for the gifts You have given me and the way that You cleanse me. Please guide me in how You would like me to serve You.

NEW MERCIES

The steadfast love of the LORD never ceases; his mercies never come
to an end; they are new every morning; great is your faithfulness.

LAMENTATIONS 3:22–23 ESV

The Lord's mercies are new every morning. As the sun rises, it lights up the tops of the mountains, and as it climbs higher in the sky, it shines upon the just and the unjust alike. Even on cloudy days and stormy days, the skies lighten. The temperature rises. Nocturnal animals bed down to sleep. Animals that are active at dawn come out. Creatures that prefer the daylight come alive, seeking food and water. Plants soak up the sun and produce oxygen through photosynthesis. The earth is alive.

God gives us a new day as well, a fresh opportunity to obey, to serve, to be faithful to what He has called us to do. We have all known days that bruised us. We've all had days when we failed. We've all had times when we fell short of who we wanted to be, of what God asked of us. We are grateful when night comes and we can close our eyes on those days! Even then, God is with us. David wrote, "On my bed I remember you; I think of you through the watches of the night. Because you are my help, I sing in the shadow of your wings" (Psalm 63:6–7). What a comforting image that is, to be in the shadow of God's wings.

How gracious God is to forgive us and to give us another day. When we are weary, another day may not feel like a gift. But Jesus said, "Come to me, all you who are weary and burdened, and I will give you rest" (Matthew 11:28).

Dear Lord, thank You for the gift of this new day You
have made. Please help me to stay close to You today.

CHOOSING A PATH

He guides me along the right paths for his name's sake.

A good path can make all the difference in an outdoor adventure. What makes a good path? Well, it's safe and properly maintained. But more importantly, it takes us someplace we want to go. Maybe it follows a geologic feature, like the Continental Divide Trail, the Pacific Crest Trail, or the Appalachian Trail. Perhaps it leads to a terrific view of the surrounding countryside, as at Clingmans Dome in the Great Smoky Mountains or Glacier Point in Yosemite. It could bring you to a stunning waterfall or meander alongside a river. Those are places worth visiting. The safest and best-kept trail in the world isn't worth a single step if it leads someplace you don't want to go.

Life can be confusing, and sometimes it's not easy to choose a direction. Our world is overflowing with information, but wisdom can be hard to find. In Psalm 25:4–5, David wrote, "Show me your ways, Lord, teach me your paths. Guide me in your truth and teach me, for you are God my Savior, and my hope is in you all day long." God answered David's prayer, for in Psalm 16, he wrote, "You make known to me the path of life; you will fill me with joy in your presence, with eternal pleasures at your right hand" (v. 11). When David's son Solomon became king, God offered to give him whatever he wanted. When Solomon asked for wisdom, God was very pleased. (See 2 Chronicles 1:7–12.)

Throughout Scripture, God promises to give wisdom to those who ask. For instance, Proverbs 2:6 says, "For the Lord gives wisdom; from his mouth come knowledge and understanding."

The best strategy for finding a good path in life is to ask for God's guidance and read the Bible. As it says in Psalm 119:105, "Your word is a lamp for my feet, a light on my path."

O Lord, You are kind and generous to Your children. Please pour out Your wisdom on me. I want to follow Your ways!

MOUNTAINS IN THE CITY

But I have calmed and quieted myself, I am like a weaned
child with its mother; like a weaned child I am content.

PSALM 131:2

Usually, we have to drive some distance to reach the mountains. But there are places where cities have grown right up around the base of a mountain, though not over it. The city of Phoenix lies on a vast, flat valley, with many mountains in the distance and several peaks within the city. South Mountain and Camelback Mountain are two that rise up within the metropolitan area.

These are not the pine-covered slopes or snowy peaks that might come to mind when we think *mountain*. The desert vegetation is sparse and hardy, so the underlying rock is what stands out from a distance. Yet they still offer much of what other mountains do. At sixteen thousand acres, South Mountain Park is the largest municipal park in the U.S. It's not one mountain, but rather three mountain ranges, and it includes more than fifty miles of trails for hiking, biking, and horseback riding. It offers amazing views of the Phoenix valley and diverse desert vegetation and wildlife. Camelback Mountain is an inspiring sight, rising in the middle of the sixth largest city in the U.S. Composed of granite and red sandstone, it is a long, rugged landform that, from the south, really does look like the head and hump of a kneeling camel.

These mountains remind us that we don't have to go far to seek God's protection and healing touch. While it's lovely to get away from it all, to have concentrated time alone with God, He often meets us amid the noise and commotion of our lives. When we turn to Him, He meets us right where we are. When we steal a moment for prayer, whether it's in our car, at our desk, or in our closet, He hears us. We can reach out for His comfort, His grace, His wisdom, and His strength. The Holy Spirit is with us there just as surely as in a remote alpine meadow.

O Lord, thank You that You meet me wherever I am. I quiet my racing mind, and I surrender to You. Please fill me with Your peace.

EAST FROM WEST

For as high as the heavens are above the earth, so great is his love for those who fear him; as far as the east is from the west, so far has he removed our transgressions from us.

PSALM 103:11–12

Sometimes we just have to get away, maybe from danger, a particular person, or even our everyday life. How far can we go? Suppose we climbed the highest mountain. The height of Mount Everest is generally given as 29,029 feet above sea level. That's a long way to go! Maybe we'd rather go halfway around the world. Going along the equator, halfway around the earth is approximately 12,450 miles.

The most challenging thing to separate ourselves from is our own sin. It is interesting to note that the psalmist, when moved by the Holy Spirit to write, did not say that God removed our sin as far as the north is from the south, but instead, as far as the east is from the west. It is so like our God to be precise. Today we know that the distance around the equator is longer than the distance around the world going over the North and South Poles.

Even more amazing is the fact that if we travel in a straight line either north or south, we eventually cross the pole and begin heading in the opposite direction. However, if we set out on a journey either true east or true west, we never end up heading the other way. God's love continually moves our sin away from us! Only the Savior who created this planet could so completely use the world to display His infinite love.

Thank You, Lord, for doing what I cannot: taking away my sin. I am so grateful! I rest in Your deep love.

PEACE AND COMFORT

"Peace I leave with you; my peace I give you. I do not give to you as the world gives. Do not let your hearts be troubled and do not be afraid."

JOHN 14:27

We often find peace in the mountains. Part of it comes merely from being away from all the distraction, the noise, the to-do lists, and the crowds. But there is more to it than that. Many people feel close to God in the mountains. Whether we're there for a short walk or a multi-week hike, we experience God's power, His creative genius, and His intimate knowledge of what we need. The Lord knew that all people would have troubled hearts. One of His ministries, throughout history, has been to comfort people.

A quick search of the words *mountain, mountains, heights,* and *hills* in a concordance or online resource shows that these high places were the location for many notable events in Scripture. Genesis 7:19 tells us the ark floated above the high mountains. Later it came to rest on Mount Ararat, where Noah found peace and the Lord was worshipped. Moses went up on Mount Sinai to receive the Ten Commandments. David hid in the mountains and wrote many psalms praising the Lord. Elijah's showdown with the priests of Baal took place on Mount Carmel.

Sadly, some people twisted the goodness of the mountains. They built places to worship false gods on high places. These were often torn down by godly kings during the Old Testament era.

Hills and mountains saw momentous events in the New Testament as well. Jesus gave rich teaching to a crowd on a mountainside; it became known as the Sermon on the Mount. Of course, the height of a hill or mountain is no measure of the events that happened there. The cross raised on a hill outside Jerusalem is the source of our forgiveness, and the empty tomb, carved into the hillside, gives us the reason for all peace.

Thank You, Lord, for the hills and mountains and all that You have done on them. Thank You for the peace that You give. Please help me to worship You in the Spirit and in truth.

LEAFY FORESTS

"Blessed is the one who trusts in the LORD, whose confidence is in him.
They will be like a tree planted by the water that sends out its roots by the
stream. It does not fear when heat comes; its leaves are always green. It
has no worries in a year of drought and never fails to bear fruit."

JEREMIAH 17:7–8

Leafy forests have an exquisite beauty all their own. In the summer, branches full of green leaves spread out against the sky. Breezes whisper gently among the leaves. Squirrels run and leap from branch to branch. Birds trill and call, many of them hidden in the foliage. The green canopy provides cool space, sheltered from the sun. Ferns grow beneath the trees. Ivies run up the trunks and along banks. Moss covers rocks and logs. It is an enchanted place.

Autumn brings a transformation to vibrant shades of red, gold, and orange. Temperatures cool. In the morning, the frost forms delicate patterns on the leaves. Everyone prepares for winter: squirrels gather seeds and other food, people cut firewood. Fallen leaves crunch underfoot until rain and fog dampen and quiet the woods.

Winter is a starker season. Tree branches are bare, revealing birds' nests that had been hidden by foliage earlier in the year. The nests sit empty now, the fledglings gone. On foggy mornings, tree trunks stand out dark in the mist. When it snows, all is covered except the trunks.

The year turns again to spring. The rains are gentle. Leaves bud on the branches. It's a noisy season, with streams running high and birds raising their young. Everywhere there is new life: flowers blooming, fish spawning in streams, and fox kits starting to explore. Life is renewed, and the cycle continues.

Thank You, Lord, for the cycle of seasons. Thank You for trees, their beauty, and their many gifts to the ecosystem. Thank You that spring always comes around again!

THE OLD MAN OF
THE MOUNTAIN

So God created mankind in his own image, in the image of
God he created them; male and female he created them.

GENESIS 1:27

Have you ever seen a face in the clouds? People have seen human faces in trees, in clouds, on the moon and Mars, and in the stars. Around the world there are rock formations that resemble faces when viewed from the right angle. One well-known example was the Old Man of the Mountain in New Hampshire. It was a granite formation on Cannon Mountain that looked like a man's profile; sadly, it crumbed and collapsed on May 3, 2003. Daniel Webster, who was born and raised in New Hampshire, had written about it, "Men hang out their signs indicative of their respective trades; shoe makers hang out a gigantic shoe; jewelers a monster watch, and the dentist hangs out a gold tooth; but up in the Mountains of New Hampshire, God Almighty has hung out a sign to show that there He makes men."

Just as we see faces in nature, we can also find some of God's attributes in the people around us. Although we are all sinful and the image of God in us is marred, there is something of His image lingering still. When we remember this, it can help us to treat one another with kindness and respect. Even those people who drive us crazy or do things we can't understand are created by God and loved by Him. Our value is rooted in the facts that God created us and loved us enough to sacrifice His Son to redeem us. It may take some effort to see His stamp on some of our fellow humans, but it is there.

Lord, thank You for making us in Your image. Help me to see Your image in those around me and to love them as You do.

BIKING

*But one thing I do: Forgetting what is behind and straining toward
what is ahead, I press on toward the goal to win the prize for
which God has called me heavenward in Christ Jesus.*

PHILIPPIANS 3:13–14

When riding a bike on mountain roads, we notice things that people in vehicles might not. Every little change in grade, either uphill or down, is felt; we may have to change gears. Small rocks or gravel, litter on the road, animals of all sizes, wind, rain, and the oncoming or passing traffic all affect those on a bike.

Of course, there are compensations for those who ride. The sights, sounds, and smells are more vivid. The exercise is good for us. There is a sense of accomplishment. Whether we're on an old single-gear Schwinn, a lightweight carbon fiber bike, a hand-driven cycle, a three-wheeler with a basket, or we're pulling a trailer, we are relying on our own power to move forward.

There are so many ways to ride: in an organized race, with a group of friends out for a weekend, spending time with the family, or maybe just you, the bike, and the mountains. Whatever the goal may be, perseverance and dedication are required. We decide how much to push, foot by foot and mile after mile. There are physical and mental obstacles, things to overcome both within ourselves and outside, that may prevent us from accomplishing what we set out to do—if we let them.

The route we take from salvation to heaven is similar. We get to decide how much we will put into it, how hard we will work, what challenges we will seek to overcome. Some people will encourage us and others will interfere. Each day we decide how much we will follow the Lord, whether we will obey or not, and the amount of ourselves we will give.

Let's imitate the apostle Paul and press on!

Father, thank You for giving me this freedom to choose how hard to push myself. Please give me the perseverance I need for this day. I want to please You on this journey.

PRAYER

"I have told you these things, so that in me you may have peace. In this
world you will have trouble. But take heart! I have overcome the world."

JOHN 16:33

It had been a hot, dry summer, so when lightning struck and forest fires began burning, no one was surprised. In the high mountains, fires raged close to a Christian youth camp. Everyone had been safely evacuated, but the lodge and cabins were threatened. Word went out to the churches in the area, and prayers surrounded the lodge for protection. When the danger had passed and the camp staff and U.S. Forest Service officials were able to get back to the camp and assess the damage, they found that everything—trees and buildings—had burned down except for the lodge. A tree at the corner of the lodge had been destroyed, and just a few scorch marks were seen on the building. But to their amazement, the lodge stood undamaged.

We are so grateful when God intervenes and gives the protection or healing that we have asked for. Yet we have all known situations where we prayed, perhaps even fasted or asked others to pray, and the result was not what we hoped for. No miracle occurred. Our hopes were crushed.

In Romans 9, Paul writes, "What then shall we say? Is God unjust? Not at all! For he says to Moses, 'I will have mercy on whom I have mercy, and I will have compassion on whom I have compassion.' It does not, therefore, depend on human desire or effort, but on God's mercy" (vv. 14–16). The truth is, we can't always know the "why" in life.

What we can rely on is that God loves us. He hears our prayers. And He will walk with us through every situation, whether it brings heartbreak or miraculous protection.

Dear Father, thank You that You hear my prayers. I don't always understand why bad things happen, but I trust Your love, Your wisdom, and Your goodness. Please fill me with Your peace.

FIRST

"But seek first his kingdom and his righteousness,
and all these things will be given to you as well."

MATTHEW 6:33

Every year people flock to climb certain mountains while other peaks nearby are virtually untouched. Why is that? Is Mount Everest or Mount Fuji or the Matterhorn or Kilimanjaro or Denali really so much better than any other summit? Certainly there are bragging rights in accomplishing a climb of "the greatest." But why do we find it necessary to go along with the crowd? How often do we spend time and treasure pursuing what others have declared to be the best, whether or not it's what we want?

Jesus knows the pride we display in being seen as the best or the greatest. He understands our hunger to acquire things and our tendency to find security in material possessions. In the Sermon on the Mount, He reminded His listeners not to worry about the everyday things of life but to look at the world around them. The birds, the flowers, and even the grass of the field are taken care of by Him. He already knows our needs. Instead of focusing on earthly treasures, we are instructed us to seek His kingdom and His righteousness.

This word *righteousness* appears more than five hundred times in the Old Testament and two hundred times in the New Testament. It concerns our ethical conduct. God is the source of all righteousness, and when we seek it, we are blessed.

So how do we cultivate righteousness in our life? The short answer is through faith. Abraham "believed God, and it was credited to him as righteousness" (Galatians 3:6; see Romans 4:3; James 2:23; and Hebrews 11). The longer answer is that we must seek it out. Proverbs 2 promises that if we search for wisdom, we will understand righteousness, justice, and equity (vv. 1–9).

Lord, please help me to seek Your kingdom and Your righteousness before all else. I want my life to be pleasing to You.

THE FATHER'S LOVE

"You have heard that it was said, 'Love your neighbor and hate your enemy.'
But I tell you, love your enemies and pray for those who persecute you, that
you may be children of your Father in heaven. He causes his sun to rise on the
evil and the good, and sends rain on the righteous and the unrighteous."

MATTHEW 5:43–45

A man from a small town had a son who was a soldier. That son was brutalized and killed in Afghanistan. The father was heartbroken. He said that he would like to meet the young men responsible. Why do you think that was?

He wanted to show them what it would be like to have someone care about them. He would take them deer hunting, take them fishing in the local rivers, and go for hikes up in the mountains—all the things he would have done with his own son. His heart was heavy with loss, but he forgave them.

This man's response was extraordinary. It also showed that he understood two things. One is that the love of an earthly dad is a powerful and precious influence. The other is that we are called to love as our heavenly Father loves.

How does He love? "This is how God showed his love among us: He sent his one and only Son into the world that we might live through him" (1 John 4:9). Romans 5:8 reminds us, "But God demonstrates his own love for us in this: While we were still sinners, Christ died for us." God loves of His own volition. He loves without our having earned it in any way. He loves so much that He sacrificed His own Son for us.

Just like the bereaved man described above, we too can pray—can *hope*—that those who wish us harm will know the unfathomable love of the Father.

Father God, I cannot understand the depths of Your love for me. Please pour Your love through me. Empower me to love others as You do, even those who are my enemies.

WATERFALLS

Deep calls to deep in the roar of your waterfalls;
all your waves and breakers have swept over me.

PSALM 42:7

So much of nature we have tamed in one way or another. We cover long distances quickly and in relative safety by car and plane. We ship food, clothing, and luxury goods by truck, train, plane, and cargo ships. Our homes protect us from the elements with sturdy roofs and reliable heating and cooling systems. Electricity puts light and heat at our command. Indoor plumbing and municipal water systems bring most of us clean water. Although we pay for these conveniences, we don't have to do hard physical work to acquire them, as many people around the world do, and as most of the world did just a few centuries ago.

Most of us are happy and grateful for this. What, if anything, have we lost by being insulated from the wild side of nature? And how do we find it again without risking our lives? We seek out beauty and grandeur in creation. We visit the ocean, the Grand Canyon, mountains, and waterfalls.

It's not difficult to find an awe-inspiring waterfall, whether it's Niagara Falls, Cumberland Falls in Kentucky, one of the falls in Yosemite National Park, or a smaller waterfall closer to home. Some waterfalls are wide but measure only inches in height, flowing smoothly over a rock lip. Others rocket down from high summits, looking string-thin from a distance because they plummet so far. Most are in between, tall and wide enough stop us in our tracks with their roar and their power. The spray nurtures plants along the banks, and when the sun is right, rainbows form in the spray. If there is space to walk behind the waterfall, we catch a glimpse of sheer abundance as water seems to pour down out of the sky.

Waterfalls are a joyous gift from our Creator. They remind us that not everything can be turned on and off with a flick of a switch, and this delights us. They bring us beauty and danger we can see and still sleep safe at night.

Thank You, my Creator, for the joy, beauty, and power of waterfalls. You are a generous and gracious God!

NATURAL DISASTERS

God has said, "Never will I leave you; never will I forsake you." So we
say with confidence, "The Lord is my helper; I will not be afraid."

Hebrews 13:5–6

We call them all natural disasters, though there is variety in how they bring destruction. In some regions, blizzards are the harshest storms, threatening life with blinding snow, impassable roads, and power outages. In other areas, springtime flooding and mudslides are more dangerous. Spring is also the heaviest tornado season, although they can happen in any month. Wildfires flare up from spring through the fall in various climates. Summer and fall bring hurricanes to the Eastern Seaboard. Earthquakes and tsunamis can happen at any time. So can volcanic eruptions, although those can sometimes be anticipated a little bit better. In each situation, volatile forces wash over us with overwhelming power and destruction. Often all we can do is try to get out of the way, try to survive them, and try to pick up the pieces after they have passed.

The fact is, no matter where we live, we all experience uncontrollable events, both in the physical world and in our personal lives. Eventually life brings days when we all feel chilled or soaked, burnt out, blown apart, or washed away. Loss, divorce, addiction, accidents, illness, the troubles of our children—you can fill in the blank. The list of life events that can knock us sideways is endless.

So how do we weather these storms? Hopefully, our family and friends gather around us. And we take shelter in the Lord. David knew what it was like to have bad days—*very* bad days. In Psalm 36 he wrote, "You, Lord, preserve both people and animals. How priceless is your unfailing love, O God! People take refuge in the shadow of your wings. . . . For with you is the fountain of life; in your light we see light" (vv. 6–7, 9). God has promised to never leave us. He is our helper, and He is utterly reliable. We may be caught in the storm, but He is there with us.

O Lord, thank You for Your shelter
in the storm. I need it! I rest in You.

GATHERING FIREWOOD

I urge, then, first of all, that petitions, prayers,
intercession and thanksgiving be made for all people.

1 TIMOTHY 2:1

Gathering firewood is a chore most campers are familiar with. One wise scout-master, when asked by a young scout how much wood he should collect, replied, "Get as much as you think you will need and put it in a pile. Then go gather the same amount and put it on the pile. Finally, go get half again the amount you have collected and add it to the wood pile. Now you have about half the amount you will need, but at least you will know where to go look for more."

Does prayer ever feel like that sort of chore? We pray and pray and pray. We wait and wait and wait for an answer. We wonder how long we need to pray before God grows weary of listening to us. What's more likely is that we will tire out long before He does. An elderly saint once said that he prayed an hour when he first arose, unless he had a lot to do that day. On those mornings, he would pray for two hours. Sounds a bit like the scoutmaster, doesn't it? However much we pray, we might want to try doubling it—and then maybe doubling it again. Paul said we should pray continually! (See 1 Thessalonians 5:16–18.)

Regardless of how we might feel, we are assured that God hears us. "I call on you, my God, for you will answer me; turn your ear to me and hear my prayer" (Psalm 17:6). God's Word would not teach us so much about prayer if it were not important. Jesus Himself gave us the pattern of the Lord's Prayer. The book of James also gives instructions about prayer, as well as the assurance that "the prayer of a righteous person is powerful and effective" (James 5:16). It is a privilege to have God's ear, and we must not take it lightly or take it for granted.

Thank You, Father, that You invite us to pray. Thank You for the examples and instructions given in Your Word. I am so grateful that You hear my prayers.

GOLD

The fear of the LORD is pure, enduring forever. The decrees of the LORD are firm,
and all of them are righteous. They are more precious than gold, than much
pure gold; they are sweeter than honey, than honey from the honeycomb.

PSALM 19:9–10

Gold has always been considered precious, and the desire for it has been a powerful motivator. Some of the most colorful and familiar examples are the North American gold rushes during the nineteenth century. "There's gold in them thar hills!" was the cry popularized during that time. Tens of thousands of prospectors streamed to the gold fields in California and the Yukon. Gold was also discovered in North Carolina, Georgia, Nevada, and South Dakota. Although some people did strike it rich panning or mining for gold, many more found the work to be dirty, strenuous, and dangerous but not profitable. Some of those who prospered most were the merchants who supplied the miners.

The Bible makes startling statements about gold—namely, that God's decrees are more precious. Do decrees sound like dry, boring laws? They are so much more. Proverbs shows that God's Word is the source of wisdom, the path to understanding. (See Proverbs 2.) It's not just about acquiring knowledge, but about discovering who God is. What is He like? What does He value? How has He made the world to function? How has He designed us to function, to flourish?

It all comes back to knowing God. His decrees reveal His character. That's why wisdom is priceless: it leads us to Him.

O Lord, I long to know You more than I long for anything
on this earth. Please draw me close to You. Let me
grow to know You and love You better and better.

PINE POLLEN

Thanks be to God, who always leads us as captives in Christ's triumphal procession and uses us to spread the aroma of the knowledge of him everywhere. For we are to God the pleasing aroma of Christ among those who are being saved and those who are perishing. To the one we are an aroma that brings death; to the other, an aroma that brings life.

2 CORINTHIANS 2:14–16

In much of the country in spring and early summer, pine pollen is everywhere. It drifts onto car windshields and forms a yellow film over puddles and ponds. Ponderosa pines are common in the western mountains, but there are about three dozen species of pine native to the United States (and more than one hundred species worldwide). Pine trees rely on the wind to carry their pollen, and in a strong breeze, clouds of it waft off the branches. It's not artificial or alien to the tree's nature; that's how the tree is designed to propagate.

In 2 Corinthians 2, we are described as spreading the aroma of the knowledge of Christ. With the influence and power of the Holy Spirit in our lives, this is as natural as the pine trees releasing pollen. We don't have to put ourselves through contortions or act weird to accomplish it. The verses don't say we slather on a fake scent; it comes naturally from being reborn in Christ.

That's not to say that everyone will like it. Just as some people are allergic to pine pollen, some may object to the aroma of the knowledge of Christ in us. That's to be expected, sad as it is.

Others will respond positively to the fragrance of Christ. Some will be drawn to it even though it is unfamiliar, and they will want to know more about our Lord. Those who already know Him will be encouraged and strengthened. When we make ourselves available, He flows through us in marvelous ways.

O Lord Jesus, I want to carry the aroma of Your presence everywhere I go. Please help me not to get in the way. I yield to You!

JOY AND JUDGMENT

Let the sea resound, and everything in it, the world, and all who live in it. Let the rivers clap their hands, let the mountains sing together for joy; let them sing before the LORD, for he comes to judge the earth. He will judge the world in righteousness and the peoples with equity.

PSALM 98:7–9

Does injustice ever make your heart ache? Do you ever weep for victims of violence, of war, of persecution or prejudice? Do these things ever make you angry?

God's justice is the answer to evil, to oppression, to those who shed innocent blood and do not fear Him. Yet Psalm 98:7–9 may sound strange to us. We don't usually talk about judgment and singing for joy in the same breath.

Even when we see the devastating effects of sin in this world, we are reluctant to ask God to bring judgment. He has been merciful to us, so we appeal to His mercy on behalf of others. We know that He is patient, "not wanting anyone to perish, but everyone to come to repentance" (2 Peter 3:9). We remember Paul, who went from persecuting Christians to becoming a leader in the early church. Surely if he could be redeemed, there's hope for anyone, right?

There is another side to God's character. Though He is patient and merciful, He is also righteous and just. God's wrath is not only an Old Testament phenomenon. Remember Jesus' words in Matthew 18: "If anyone causes one of these little ones—those who believe in me—to stumble, it would be better for them to have a large millstone hung around their neck and to be drowned in the depths of the sea" (v. 6).

As the Holy Spirit transforms us to be more like Christ, it's natural that we grow heartsick at the corruption and spiritual death all around us. Looking forward to God's judgment does not mean we take joy in destruction. Rather, we long for restoration, for everything to be made right.

Almighty God, I am so grateful that You are both merciful and just.
Some days, the rottenness in this world breaks my heart and fills me with
discouragement. I look forward to the day that You bring restoration.

WASHING DISHES

*In a large house there are articles not only of gold and silver, but also of wood
and clay; some are for special purposes and some for common use. Those who
cleanse themselves from the latter will be instruments for special purposes,
made holy, useful to the Master and prepared to do any good work.*

2 TIMOTHY 2:20–21

What kind of dishes do you take when you go camping? It probably depends on what sort of camping you do. There are a lot more options out there than speckled blue enamel dishes and Coleman stoves!

There are a couple of ideas to consider. First, how much do you want to carry? Obviously, there's a big difference in how much you might want to carry if you're driving an RV with half a dozen people, or if you're backpacking and each person carries his own kitchen gear. And second, how will you wash them? Are you hooking up to power and water in an RV park? Boiling a pot of water on a Coleman stove? Or mostly using paper plates that are burned in the campfire?

In his second letter to Timothy, Paul compared us to dishes. He suggested that if we cleanse ourselves, we will be ready and prepared for whatever the Lord asks us to do.

So how do we cleanse ourselves? Many passages in the Bible describe cleansing as something that the Lord does for us. In 1 John we read, "If we walk in the Light as He Himself is in the Light, we have fellowship with one another, and the blood of Jesus His Son cleanses us from all sin. . . . If we confess our sins, He is faithful and righteous to forgive us our sins and to cleanse us from all unrighteousness" (1:7, 9 NASB). We can yield to the Lord's cleansing. He will do a wiser, gentler, more thorough job of it than we ever could!

O Lord, I want to be ready for whatever You call me to do. Please gently point out where I need cleansing. Forgive me, cleanse me, and prepare me for what lies ahead.

LOST AND FOUND

"For the Son of Man came to seek and to save the lost."

LUKE 19:10

We hear the stories of people lost in the mountains. Some were hiking; others were out for a drive. Often the weather was bad or darkness was settling in. Sometimes things didn't end well; other times it was as though something or Someone was guiding the search and rescue team. We wonder why one lost person is found and another is not. It's one of life's many mysteries. We realize, even when we don't stop to think about it, that life here on earth is temporary.

That's one of the reasons we have a desire to worship. Our longing for God is satisfied only by God, though we so often try to appease it with other things. "Since the creation of the world God's invisible qualities—his eternal power and divine nature—have been clearly seen, being understood from what has been made, so that people are without excuse" (Romans 1:20). Similarly, "The heavens declare the glory of God; the skies proclaim the work of his hands. . . . They have no speech, they use no words; no sound is heard from them. Yet their voice goes out into all the earth, their words to the ends of the world" (Psalm 19:1, 3–4).

When we hear His voice and yield to Him, we receive salvation as just the first of many blessings (John 3:16; Revelation 3:20). There are many other promises as well; here are a few of them. Jesus came so that we "may have life and have it abundantly" (John 10:10 ESV). He forgives our sin (Jeremiah 31:34; 36:3; Acts 3:19; and many more). He has sent the Holy Spirit to be our Comforter and Counselor (John 14:26 AMP). He is always with us (Isaiah 41:10; Matthew 28:20).

When the Lord finds us, He changes our lives in so many ways!

O Lord, You are the Holy One, my Creator and my Redeemer.
I worship You. Thank You for Your many gifts!

SOLACE

Your love, LORD, reaches to the heavens, your faithfulness to the skies.
Your righteousness is like the highest mountains, your justice like the
great deep. You, LORD, preserve both people and animals.

PSALM 36:5–6

Our culture celebrates challenge and achievement, so mountains are often marketed as something to conquer, whether by climbing, biking, skiing, or snowmobiling. And those are all terrific pursuits. But sometimes life is already throwing plenty of challenges our way, and it's solace we seek from being outdoors.

Hiking a trail through the woods can help us to heal a little bit. The sounds of a stream running over rocks is a balm to our battered soul. When we've lost a loved one, eating lunch with friends at a lakeside restaurant cheers us. Sitting on a bench in the sunshine warms not only our body but our spirit too. Seeing wildflowers in bloom reminds us what beauty looks like and how delight feels. Hiking can help burn off the energy of anger. Waterfalls reawaken our sense of awe. The challenge of birding distracts us and gives us the joy of discovery. The sound of wind in the trees lifts our spirits. Hunting and fishing offer the healing of quiet solitude in the country, the camaraderie of friends in camp, and perhaps the satisfaction of providing food for the table. When we camp in the backcountry, the dark and the quiet seep into our bones, and we relax more deeply than we thought possible. These are just a few of the kinds of comfort we often find in the wild country.

Why is it so calming, so healing to come to the mountains? God made us for them and them for us. He created this world. He is reflected in the variety of places and the sorts of wonder and joy they bring us. God is infinite, not just in power and knowledge, but also in His creativity. Although the environment has been marred by the activities of sinful humanity, it still reveals to us the beauty and the nurturing heart of our Creator.

Father God, I love this earth that You have created.
Thank You especially for the mountains and the
way they heal my soul. I am so grateful!

FAITH, HOPE, AND CHARITY

And now abideth faith, hope, charity, these three; but the greatest of these is charity.

1 CORINTHIANS 13:13 KJV

Many people say they love the mountains. In Central Oregon there is a mountain named for love. The early settlers crossing the high desert could see the mountains grow larger each day as they traveled west. Perhaps someone was reading 1 Corinthians 13 as the early morning sun revealed the mountains that today are commonly known as the Three Sisters. Someone named them—from north to south—Faith, Hope, and Charity. And indeed, the largest—or greatest—of these impressive snowcapped peaks is South Sister, Charity. The promise of year-round pure water from the melting snow may have reminded a weary traveler of God's love and provision for us. Today in that area there is a water bottling plant and an extensive canal system that waters thousands of acres of farms.

In many passages of Scripture, water is compared to the Word of God or to the spiritual cleansing that comes with salvation. In John 4, a Samaritan woman went to the well for water and learned of One who can quench our spiritual thirst. Like her, we can go to the Word and find refreshment.

Whether we simply gaze at the mountains or spend days wandering through them, we are aware of their majesty. There we may find solitude, peace, or even an answer to what is troubling our soul. God's creation was designed for our benefit. When we combine Scripture with the outdoors, we are doubly blessed. We begin to understand why many biblical accounts take place in the wildlands. God's love for us is seen in His provision of fellowship and solitude, in flatland and steep hillsides, in deserts, forests, mountains, and everything in between. He is so good to us.

O Lord, thank You for Your love. You are the only One who can fully satisfy my spiritual thirst. Please let me remember to seek You often.

CREATOR OF THE WILD

"The wild animals honor me, the jackals and the owls, because I
provide water in the wilderness and streams in the wasteland."

ISAIAH 43:20

God created the mountains. How wonderful are His designs! He shaped the ridges and the peaks. He robed them with trees and trimmed them with vines. He designed the streams, the pools, the waterfalls. He provided homes for His creatures: deer and foxes, bobcats and bears, fish and salamanders, bats and fireflies. Not to mention the birds: eagles and owls, ducks and geese, herons and kingfishers, hummingbirds and chickadees, mourning doves and warblers, cardinals and sparrows. He sees each den and every nest. He knows where the flowers bloom and the berries grow.

The air is cool and fresh. The sun is bright, and the weather is unpredictable. Rain and fog come unannounced. The wild and beautiful mountains belong to God. Here the rugged land reminds us that we do not command everything we see. There are places we have not tamed, just as God cannot be tamed. The mountains offer us a tiny glimpse of their Creator: His power, His strength, His grandeur and majesty. We are reminded that we are small. We are finite; He is infinite. We have a few short years on this earth; He is eternal. We see just our own little experience and point of view. He sees all; nothing is hidden from Him, nothing overlooked.

We are refreshed by the mountains. They remind us where we fit into the big picture. We are not the Divine Artist. We are not tasked with carrying the weight of the world on our shoulders. We need only to run our own race and trust God's power and goodness beyond all.

O Lord, thank You for the wild places still left on the earth. Thank You for watering the earth with rain and bringing forth abundance. Your creation refreshes me!